A STUDENT'S GUIDE TO SELF-CARE

**Daniel S. Testa and
Varunee Faii Sangganjanavanich**

cognella® | ACADEMIC PUBLISHING

Bassim Hamadeh, CEO and Publisher

Kassie Graves, Acquisitions Editor

Berenice Quirino, Associate Production Editor

Miguel Macias, Senior Graphic Designer

Alexa Lucido, Licensing Associate

Don Kesner, Interior Designer

Natalie Piccotti, Senior Marketing Manager

Kassie Graves, Director of Acquisitions and Sales

Jamie Giganti, Senior Managing Editor

Cover image: Copyright © 2015 iStockphoto LP/g-stockstudio.

Printed in the United States of America.

ISBN: 978-1-5165-1658-2 (pbk)

cognella® | ACADEMIC PUBLISHING

A STUDENT'S GUIDE TO SELF-CARE

THE COGNELLA SERIES ON STUDENT SUCCESS

Student success isn't always measured in straight As.

Many students arrive at college believing that if they study hard and earn top grades, their higher education experience will be a success. Few recognize that some of their greatest learning opportunities will take place outside the classroom. Learning how to manage stress, navigate new relationships, or put together a budget can be just as important as acing a pop quiz.

The Cognella Series on Student Success is a collection of books designed to help students develop the essential life and learning skills needed to support a happy, healthy, and productive higher education experience. Featuring topics suggested by students and books written by experts, the series offers research-based, yet practical advice to help any student navigate new challenges and succeed throughout their college experience.

Series Editor: Richard Parsons, Ph.D.
Professor of Counselor Education, West Chester University

Other titles available in the series:

- *A Student's Guide to Stress Management*
- *A Student's Guide to a Meaningful Career*
- *A Student's Guide to College Transition*
- *A Student's Guide to Money Matters*
- *A Student's Guide to Communication and Self-Presentation*
- *A Student's Guide to Exercise for Improving Health*

ABOUT THE AUTHORS

T he transition from high school to college can be a difficult one, full of new experiences, stressful demands, and important choices. As you navigate this big life change, it's easy to lose track of the one thing you should always strive to take care of—yourself.

A Student's Guide to Self-Care provides you with simple, effective ways to think about and live a healthier lifestyle as you settle in to college life. The guide offers you a holistic approach to self-care, presenting research and best practices you can easily apply to your daily life to foster mental, emotional, and physical well-being throughout your academic career.

Full of practical suggestions and activities, this guide will help you develop a happy and healthy lifestyle that will benefit you not only during your college years, but well beyond them.

A Student's Guide to Self-Care is part of the Cognella Series on Student Success, a collection of books designed to help students develop the essential life and learning skills needed to support a happy, healthy, and productive higher education experience.

Daniel S. Testa is a Licensed Professional Mental Health Counselor with supervisor endorsement at the United States Department of Veterans Affairs and in the state of Ohio. Dr. Testa earned his master's degree in clinical counseling from Malone University and his doctoral degree in counselor education and supervision from The University of Akron.

Varunee Faii Sangganjanavanich is a professor and interim director of the School of Counseling at The University of Akron. She is a Licensed Professional Clinical Counselor with supervisor endorsement in the state of Ohio. Dr. Sangganjanavanich earned her master's in human sexuality from Chulalongkorn University and her doctoral degree in counselor education and supervision from the University of Northern Colorado.

CONTENTS

EDITOR'S PREFACE

T he transition to college marks a significant milestone in a person's life. Many of you will be preparing to live away from your friends and family for the very first time. Clearly this is and should be an exciting time.

It is a time to experience new things and experiment with new options. While the opportunity to grow is clear—so too are the many challenges you will experience as you transition from high school to college.

Research suggests that the first year of college is the most difficult period of adjustment a student faces. Not only will you be required to adjust to new academic demands but you will also have to navigate a number of social and emotional challenges that accompany your life as a college student. The books found within this series—*Cognella Series on Student Success*—have been developed to help you with the many issues confronting your successful transition from life as a high school student to life as a collegiate. Each book within the series was designed to provide research-based, yet *practical* advice to assist you succeeding in your college experience.

We live in a culture that seems to emphasize competition, productivity, and achievement above all else. While such a focus can be healthy and effective for the creation of an enjoyable life, sometimes it is achieved at a significant cost to one's health and well-being. The current book, *A Student's Guide to Self-Care*, provides an antidote to the "rat race" mentality—that perspective that puts one's own self and well-being at the bottom of the "things to do list."

This is not to suggest that the goal of the book is to foster a non-caring, feet-up approach to life. No, as you will see in the upcoming pages, *Caring for Self* can be "hard work." It is, however, the type of work, or intentional focus, that will not only improve your physical health, your interpersonal relationships, and your general experience of life but it will also position you to truly perform and achieve at your optimal levels while maintaining your overall well-being.

A Student's Guide to Self-Care provides well-researched, practical advice for developing skills essential to maintaining your health, your happiness, and your well-being. As with all of the books in this series, the information provided has been drawn from established theory and empirical research. However, it is important to note that this is NOT a textbook (you have enough of those), nor is it intended to be an academic text. Rather, this book, as is true for all the books in the series, has been written to be a useful guide for the reader. To this end, the authors will help you see the practical value of the information shared through their use of numerous case illustrations in a feature called *"Voices From Campus."* In addition to understanding the concepts presented as well as their application by way of the case illustrations, you will be invited to apply what you learn by way of a feature called *"Your Turn."*

The integration of solid information with a format that encourages your own personal application makes this book, as well as the other books within the series, a useful guide to your successful transition from high school to college.

Richard Parsons, Ph.D.
Series Editor

AUTHORS' PREFACE

Y ou may have just started to enjoy your high school experience and then, the next thing you know, you are going to college. Being a college student requires you to transition from high school to a new and uncharted journey—so-called college life. There is no question that college life is difficult and may push you to take a look at your life differently. College life also requires you to spend your internal and external resources in order to be successful. At times, this can become very exhausting.

A Student's Guide to Self-Care offers you ways to think about how you can attend to your self-care needs and live a healthier life. This book is designed to help you manage and cope with transitioning from high school to college and the challenges that you may face. The book is informed by the latest research and best practices in the biological, psychological, and social sciences. The aim is to provide a holistic approach to self-care by addressing your emotional, psychological, and biological needs.

Practical suggestions are presented to you through a variety of formats which allow you to engage with the material on an individual level and tailor strategies to your own needs. The exercises involved in each chapter are meant to help you understand and reflect on where problems develop and how you can maneuver through them. Each chapter ends with a unique story that attempts to capture the material in the chapter. The stories are an attempt to reflect the realities of college life and the hardships that await.

Finally, we encourage you to use the material presented in this text as a foundation for not just taking care of yourself as you go through college, but also as you encounter obstacles and life challenges beyond your college years. The choices you make toward your health now can have effects long past receiving your college diploma. Self-care is not a set of "how to's." It is a style of living that takes practice and commitment. Remember that self-care is hard—some days you are motivated to take care of yourself and other days you may struggle to do so. It is an ebb and flow—a give-and-take process—and we are honored to be a part of this self-care journey with you.

ADJUSTING TO COLLEGE LIFE

So here you are. You successfully graduated high school, and now you are on your way to a new chapter in your life—college. This is an incredibly exciting time for you as you transition from one level of education to another. There is more freedom and independence that comes with being a college student. This can be a welcomed change from the constant monitoring from teachers and parents during high school. Some of you are leaving home for the very first time, which means you will have endless opportunities to meet new people and try different things. Personally, this is an opportunity for you to develop your identity and define your life goals and values. It is an opportunity to understand your personal, professional, and academic potential. This is a time when you begin to shed old roles and start investing in new ones.

For some of you, this may be an overwhelming and scary experience. You are now faced with completely new educational and personal demands. As you mourn the loss of childhood, you are expected to function more independently and responsibly. For example, you must learn to manage your finances and take care of your basic needs such as cooking and washing clothes. You also must learn how to navigate your campus' rules and regulations on your own. Compared to your high school, college campuses are more heterogeneous, meaning they are made up of individuals with diverse cultural backgrounds. In high school, you may have been used to class sizes of 30 students. In college, you may be attending classes that have 200 students. That can be more than your entire high school graduating class. Along with being exposed to more diversity in the classroom, you must learn how to adjust to each instructor's teaching style and expectations. Managing deadlines and exam schedules in multiple courses can feel daunting. If you are a nonresidential student, leaving home can be a difficult adjustment as you separate from friends and family, leaving old support systems behind. This can lead to feelings of loneliness, homesickness, and grief.

It is important to remember that these experiences are a normal process of adjusting to campus life. To get you ahead of the game, we will discuss some factors that will enable you to transition successfully into your freshman year at college. The first factor is self-efficacy—your belief in your ability to develop and carry out a plan of action to achieve a certain goal. Let's say that you want to start a specific social action club on campus and help plan events. How will you recruit members? How do you envision yourself being a leader? What personal skills will lend to the success of the group? Another way to think of self-efficacy is your level of confidence in yourself. If you have more confidence, you are more willing to initiate tasks, put in the extra effort, and try to achieve a sense of mastery in your work. This will be fundamental in your coursework and studies. If you have more motivation for accomplishment, you will focus on personal goals of higher academic achievement which require dedication to studying.

A second factor is developing your ability to learn on your own. As a college freshman, you will be expected to you work more independently and adjust to each instructor's teaching methods. Learning how to manage your time, meeting deadlines, and developing successful study habits will be essential in helping you stay motivated and feel as though you are in control.

A third factor which will be important in your transition is how closely connected you feel to your college environment. This is known as social integration. The importance of developing and cultivating a strong social support network during your freshman year cannot be emphasized enough. Faculty, staff, and peers can be a great resource in helping you adjust to this new lifestyle, so it is best to start reaching out and developing these relationships sooner rather than later. As you connect with faculty, staff, and peers, you have more opportunities to be involved with campus activities. Also, these individuals can offer emotional support outside of your family. One of the social challenges in becoming a young adult is learning how to build harmonious relationships and resolve interpersonal conflicts. This will be a constant challenge as you navigate new relationships both with friends and romantic connections. Fostering relationships with faculty can also assist you in developing and achieving academic and intellectual goals.

YOUR TURN 1.1

My Challenges and Obstacles

Directions: Below is a list of many of the obstacles you may encounter and adjustments that you may have to make as you begin your freshman year in college. Review the list and select the items which you think will present the most challenge for you. After you are finished, identify some possible resources that could help you overcome those challenges. You may select multiple resources for a given challenge.

Challenge/Obstacle:

_____ Moving away from home

Resource(s):

_____

_____

_____ Leaving behind family

Resource(s):

_____

_____

_____ Leaving behind friends

Resource(s):

_____

_____

_____ Managing finances

Resource(s):

_____

_____

_____ Taking care of basic needs

Resource(s):

_____

_____

_____ Course load

Resource(s):

_____

_____

_____ Finding full-/part-time work

Resource(s):

_____

_____

_____ Childcare

Resource(s):

_____

_____

_____ Meeting new people

Resource(s):

_____

_____

_____ Understanding campus policies and procedures

Resource(s):

_____

_____

_____ Developing romantic relationship

Resource(s):

_____

_____

_____ Studying

Resource(s):

_____

_____

_____ Peer pressure(s)

Resource(s):

_____

_____

_____ Isolation

Resource(s):

_____

_____

_____ Joining campus groups

Resource(s):

_____

_____

_____ Attending classes

Resource(s):

_____

_____

_____ Completing assignments

Resource(s):

_____

_____

_____ Living with roommates

Resource(s):

_____

_____

_____ Lecture formats during class

Resource(s):

_____

_____

_____ Larger class sizes

Resource(s):

_____

_____

_____ Collaborating/networking with faculty

Resource(s):

_____

_____

_____ Managing stress

Resource(s):

_____

_____

_____ Time management

Resource(s):

_____

_____

Possible Resources: Campus health or wellness center, counseling center, faculty, peers, parents, friends, social media/technology, academic advising, tutoring/writing centers, library, career services, spiritual life office, student clubs/organizations, intramural sports, student center/union, legal service center, student accessibility office, residence assistant (RA), social clubs

Tool Box 1.1

- College represents the first significant milestone in your adult life.
- Adjusting to campus life will bring many unique personal and academic challenges.
- Successful transition from high school to college involves developing self-efficacy, effective learning strategies, and social integration.

Did You Know?

- Common factors that affect adjusting to college among first-year students include shyness, fear of failure/disapproval, loneliness, and homesickness.
- Avoidance can be a common coping mechanism to deal with challenges adjusting to university life.
- Although socializing is a healthy way to cope and adjust to your first year in college, it is becoming more difficult for college freshmen. In 1987, 38 percent of incoming college students socialized at least 16 hours per week. That number decreased to 18 percent in 2014.

VOICES FROM CAMPUS 1.1

Lost at Sea

I came from a small high school about five hours away from where I decided to go to college. Even though my school was small, I developed a few close relationships. We had a tight-knit group. I was not the loner type, but I also would never have been considered for homecoming queen—a title I was comfortable not having.

When I crash landed on campus, I remember feeling paralyzed and dazed by the sheer amount of people around me. Just an endless sea of faces passing by. Every face you saw was a new person. It seemed as though most people already knew each other. That or most of the people in my dorm wanted to party, which was just not my scene. I ended up quickly feeling distant from everyone else. My first week on campus was spent in bed with my door shut while I refreshed my Instagram and checked Facebook updates from friends back home who were posting about a fun social event they attended the previous night. I felt like I was just doing nothing all the time.

My first day was a complete disaster. I tossed and turned all night dwelling on what the next day would bring. I was so focused on the next day that I forgot to set my alarm. Luckily, there was no scarcity of noise in the hallway to wake me up. I swear you would have thought it was a herd of animals sometimes. I rushed out to my first class barely making it on time. I remember feeling sheer panic when I walked into my class and saw a sea of students in a large lecture auditorium. So much panic that I walked right back out the door and went to the nearest bathroom to calm down. I must have sat in the bathroom stall for 45 minutes. Eventually, I would spend more moments there, cupping my face in shame while holding back tears. Over time, I became particularly attached to that bathroom stall.

I became increasingly homesick and developed what I later found out was called the "freshman blues." I cannot begin to imagine how many times I cried during my first semester. I cried in the bathroom, and I cried in my room. I cried when I woke up in the morning and sometimes cried myself to sleep. I could not understand why I was having such a difficult time. Why was it so hard for me to make friends when it was so easy for me back home? When the anxiety or depression hit, it felt like it impacted everything. I had problems eating and getting out of bed. This made it impossible for me to attend class and study.

I had to learn that just because someone lives in the same room or down the hall, it does not mean you will be kindred spirits. It took a while for me to meet people and eventually build relationships. Even though there is still a stigma of going to counseling out there, I decided to make an appointment at my counseling center. I was initially afraid that counseling would validate my fear that I was crazy or something was wrong with me. That could not have been any farther from the truth. I learned that I was not crazy and that what I was experiencing was normal. This felt like a huge weight had been lifted from me. My counselor and I worked through what was causing me to get stuck and feel discouraged from making new friends. He helped me connect with other campus resources and activities which allowed me to take better care of myself and to meet other people.

You never see or hear about the awkwardness that comes with starting college. You only hear about how quickly you will make new friends or how easy your classes will be. Movies and television bombard you with this image of college life composed of parties, checking out peers during class, morning hangovers, and meeting an attractive person as they accidentally bump into you from catching a frisbee on the quad.

The truth is that my story is more common that what you see on your TV. It is completely fine to be excited about what college has to offer. Just do not think it will be an easy transition. Most importantly, if I had one piece of advice to share it would be to get out of the bathroom stall and talk to a professional. Reach out for support before you start drifting too far out, and you end up lost at sea.

UNDERSTANDING STRESS

Before we begin to delve into the focus of this book, it is important that we shift our attention briefly to an important topic—stress. It may be a difficult reality to accept, but stress will be an inevitable experience as you move throughout your college career. It is unavoidable. The sooner you accept this reality, the sooner you can begin to develop a plan to counter and reduce stress in your life. This will enable you to have a more rewarding college experience. This chapter will help you learn about the different types of stress you may encounter throughout college. We will also discuss warning signs and symptoms of each type of stress. For a more thorough discussion of stress, we encourage you to read another book in this series titled *A Student's Guide to Managing Stress.*

2.1: Types of Stress

As you move through your college experience, you will most likely encounter various types of stress. Each type of stress has its own symptoms and characteristics along with ways to cope with each form. Remember—stress is inevitable so let's take some time to identify each type. Being able to identify the type of stress will enable you to take proactive measures to reduce or eliminate the symptoms. The rest of this book will be dedicated to developing a plan on how to take care of yourself when stress occurs.

The first type of stress is known as acute stress. You will most likely experience this type of stress frequently throughout college. Acute stress occurs when there are anticipated demands and pressures of the near future. Some common examples of this may be trying to finish a term paper or cramming for a final exam the night before it is due. Other acute stressors that you may run into include getting a flat tire on your way to work, being turned down for an internship, or research deadlines. The defining feature of this type of stress is that it is acute—meaning that the duration is short and usually comes with minimal effects on your mental and physical health.

There are times when acute stressors can seem to clump up together, or you notice them occurring more frequently. This is known as episodic acute stress. People who experience this type of stress are often described as being irritable, anxious, and tense. This is due in large part to their personality known as "Type A." Individuals who exhibit Type A personalities are known to be very competitive. Due to their competitive nature, their lives often take on a sense of urgency. They may find themselves rushing all of the time and still managing to be late. These individuals often take on too much work and have difficulty organizing the unrealistic or unreasonable demands of their life. Have you ever been described as a "worry wart?" Well, this is another personality style that often is related to episodic acute stress. Individuals who excessively worry can be pessimistic. They tend to "awfulize" situations, believing that every situation will end in catastrophe. These individuals find themselves feeling more anxious, depressed, angry, and hostile.

Finally, there is a more severe and life-threatening form of stress known as chronic stress. Whereas acute stress and episodic acute stress are relatively short in duration, chronic stress is a debilitating condition in which a person seems to suffer day in and day out. This type of stress can go on for years if untreated, and often the individual will become accustomed to this style of living.

YOUR TURN 2.1

My Stressors

Directions: Take some time to identify the situations in which you become stressed. What do you notice? Are you more prone to physical, psychological, or emotional types of stressors?

Physical:
___manual labor   ___lack of sleep   ___traveling   ___illness
___injury/burns   ___infection   ___surgery   ___overexertion
___hormonal or biochemical imbalance   ___food allergies
___vitamin deficiency

Chemical:
___drugs   ___alcohol   ___caffeine   ___nicotine   ___environmental
chemicals or pesticides   ___environmental pollutants

Mental:
___self-criticism   ___ sense of lack of control   ___information
overload   ___worry   ___sense of lack of time   ___long work
hours   ___perfectionism

Emotional:
___anxiety   ___anger   ___sadness   ___depression   ___fears
___grief/bereavement   ___shame   ___loneliness   ___insecurity

Social–Spiritual:
___financial/lack of money   ___career pressure   ___lack of meaning
or purpose   ___lack of values   ___disconnected from one's self
___troubled relationships   ___isolation   ___pessimistic view of self,
others, or world

Tool Box 2.1

- Stress is an inevitable experience of college life.
- There are three main types of stress: acute, episodic, and chronic.
- Each have their own defining symptoms and methods of treatment.

Did You Know?

- More than 30 percent of college freshmen report feeling overwhelmed a great deal of the time.
- 75 percent of individuals with an anxiety disorder are diagnosed before the age of 22.

2.2: Signs and Symptoms

Although the effects are minimal, acute stress can be recognized by a variety of symptoms. You may notice emotional distress in the form of anxiety, anger, or irritability. Physical problems may manifest in the form of muscle tension and migraines or headaches. In addition to these physical problems, you may notice gastrointestinal symptoms such as heartburn, acid reflux, diarrhea, constipation, or irritable bowel syndrome. Symptoms of acute stress can also mimic those of panic/anxiety attacks which include elevated blood pressure, shortness of breath, chest pain, increased heart rate, and dizziness.

There are several symptoms that accompany episodic acute stress. These symptoms include persistent tension headaches, migraines, hypertension, chest pain, and heart disease. There are long periods of depression, anxiety, and emotional distress. The hallmark characteristic is that these symptoms, more specifically, ceaseless worrying, extend over a longer period. Episodic acute stress is due to personality and lifestyle issues. Long-term effects of episodic stress may include insomnia, weight change, and frequent illnesses due to a weakened immune system. You may notice difficulties concentrating, low productivity, negative attitude, and forgetfulness. This can make treatment more difficult since individuals can be resistant to change. Since episodic acute stress affects your physical and mental health, it is recommended that you talk with both a physician and mental health provider to address the symptoms and underlying issues creating the stress.

Individuals who are suffering from chronic stress find themselves in misery. They detest and hate their jobs, or they are unhappy in their relationships or marriage. These individuals may have experienced a traumatic event in the past which has been left untreated. Chronic stress can be the result of the stress of living in poverty or dealing with a chronic illness. Individuals suffering from chronic stress feel trapped in an endless cycle of dysfunction which affects their lives at work, school, or at home. These individuals become so used to this way of life that they can be described as hopeless because they see no way out of the constant demands that never seem to end.

What makes this condition deadly is the toll the stress takes on a person's body and mental health. This toll can lead to fatal consequences such as a heart attack or stroke. Individuals with chronic stress are also at risk for increased suicide or violence against others. Due to the significant health complications and severity of symptoms, it is highly recommended that you seek medical and mental health treatment if you are experiencing chronic stress.

YOUR TURN 2.2

My College Stressors

Directions: Now that we have talked about the types of stress and their symptoms let us review the many ways in which stress can occur as you start your freshman year. Identify which items may contribute to your own stress. Is it an acute stress? If it is not managed correctly, could it turn into an episodic or chronic stressor?

___Picking a major   ___Did I make the right choice?   ___Learning how to study   ___Challenging courses   ___Deciding on a career   ___Credits/paperwork   ___Maintaining high grades/GPA___Conflict with instructor(s)   ___Finding a job   ___Finding an internship   __Balancing work and courses ___Fired from a job ___Tuition ___Death of a spouse ___Maintaining scholarship(s) ___Paying bills ___Finding time for family ___Expectations and pressures from family ___Sick relative ___Divorce ___Death of a close friend ___Finding time for friends ___Peer pressures ___Dating ___Unwed pregnancy ___Living independently ___Learning to live with roommates ___Being away from home ___Substance use ___Jail/incarceration ___Death of a parent ___Developing sexuality identity/orientation ___Living in a new city ___Missing old friends ___Culture shock

Tool Box 2.2

- Acute stress is identified by minimal symptoms that mimic those of panic attacks. Other physical symptoms may occur that are gastrointestinal.
- Episodic acute stress is due to personality and lifestyle issues.
- Chronic stress is a persistent illness which can have life-threatening consequences.

Did You Know?

- The stigma of mental health treatment is the number one barrier to college students.

2.3: Burnout

One of the major challenges in college is learning what your limits are when it comes to how much physical, mental, and emotional energy you can spend without needing to recharge. College will undoubtedly test these limits. Often, you may feel as though you are just "running on empty"—that you have very little or no energy to complete tasks or accomplish your goals. If you find yourself in this constant cycle of depleting energy while your own needs are not being met, you may be experiencing burnout.

Burnout is usually associated with experiencing three specific symptoms: emotional exhaustion, depersonalization, and a lack of personal accomplishment. The first symptom would be emotional exhaustion. This occurs when your emotional resources are depleted. Eventually, you are not able to accomplish tasks and goals. You find yourself feeling extremely tired and you lack energy. When this exhaustion occurs, you will naturally act to conserve what little energy you have left. To conserve your energy, you may find yourself slowly withdrawing mentally and emotionally from your studies. For example, you may be having constant fights with your partner and family members. As a result, you are distracted in class or have little motivation to accomplish assignments or deadlines.

The second criterion of burnout is called depersonalization. This occurs when you start feeling detached from those around you. More specifically, you have a more negative and distant attitude about people, usually those who you are close with. You may also feel cynical toward the material you are learning in your courses. This cynicism is viewed as a coping response to protect yourself from further depleting your emotional reserves.

The last major criteria for burnout is feeling a lack of personal accomplishments. You can begin to develop a sense of feeling increasingly incompetent and unable to fulfill your academic responsibilities. When you are experiencing burnout, you may evaluate yourself and your achievements more harshly or negatively. This results in fewer achievements and not being as productive. For example, you may have aced your organic chemistry final but are unable to celebrate or be excited because you feel you could have done better or are just indifferent altogether about your grade.

As a freshman in college, you are susceptible to a wide variety of pressures. These pressures are associated with achievements (e.g., high GPA, grades, sports). To reach these achievements, you may feel as though you have to compete with those around you. Competition has its benefits—it can motivate you, challenge you to think in new and innovative ways, and push you outside your comfort zone. However, too much competition can have long-term effects on your mental and physical health. Instead of learning how to cooperate with others, you find yourself having to surpass others. Without the correct resources and healthy coping skills, you become at risk for developing burnout.

Utilizing resources and developing positive coping skills can help you build resiliency toward stress and burnout. Resilience is often discussed along with stress and burnout. Resilience refers to your ability to success-fully cope, overcome, and adapt to difficult situations or adversity in your life. When you develop resiliency to your environment, you are drawing on your own support systems and strengths. These support systems can be both internal and external. For example, internal support systems include coping skills and self-esteem or self-efficacy. External resources include support from friends or family. The result includes maintaining your psychological and physical health. One of the primary goals of this book is to help you identify which external and internal resources are important for you and how you can develop them in your own life. Doing so will help you cultivate a natural resilience to the stresses of college life.

YOUR TURN 2.3

Understanding My Resiliency

Directions: Below is a list of common external and internal resilience factors. Take some time to review each one. Rate them in regards to their level of importance to you and how strong you feel they are at this moment in your life by putting a checkmark in the appropriate box.

	Level of importance in your life			How strong is each factor in your life at this moment?		
Internal Factors	Not important	Somewhat important	Very important	Not strong at all	Somewhat strong	Very strong
Commitment to learning						
Positive values						
Empathy towards others						
Resistance to peer pressure						

	Level of importance in your life				How strong is each factor in your life at this moment?		
Internal Factors	Not important	Somewhat important	Very important		Not strong at all	Somewhat strong	Very strong
Self-esteem							
Self-efficacy							
Self-control							
Planning and decision making							
Cultural awareness							
Acceptance							
Spirituality							
Caring							
Goals							
Self-awareness							
Optimism							
External Factors							
Family support							
High expectations							
Positive peer relationships							
Caring school climate							
Caring neighborhood							
Adult relationships							
Opportunities to participate and contribute							
Positive mentors							
Religion/church							

Tool Box 2.3

- Burnout is associated with emotional exhaustion, depersonalization, and a lack of personal accomplishment.
- Burnout can be a result of intense competition that is fostered on campus.
- Developing resilience can help protect against symptoms of stress and burnout.

2.4: Did You Know?

- Factors that lead students to withdraw from their studies include financial difficulties, transferring to another university, family responsibilities, personal problems, and dissatisfaction with courses.
- High rates of stress levels among college freshmen are usually associated with oral presentations, taking exams, taking too many classes, and a lack of time to meet commitments.
- You are more likely to complete your first year of college if you have a clear reason for attending college and know the type of occupation you hope to achieve.

VOICES FROM CAMPUS 2.1

Out of My Element

I grew up in a violent neighborhood. My mother worked two jobs to pay the bills all while being a single mother. She taught me early on that to succeed I would have to do this on my own. I would have to be the one to push myself beyond my limits. My teachers and peers were all supportive of me as I pushed myself to become a straight-A student. This was a monumental achievement considering only 20 percent of my school, comprising Latinos and blacks, was proficient in English. I was voted most likely to succeed, and with the help of scholarships, grants, and programs, I was accepted to a highly renowned university. I was on my way—on my way to make my mother proud and to not become another statistic or stereotype.

When I arrived on campus my first week, it was a culture shock. My school set up a program for black first-year students called the Black Cultural Society. The goal of the program was to help build bonds with other black freshmen and help remind us of home and our families. Although this was a positive step for the school, it did not help that African Americans were becoming a declining minority on campus. To put this in perspective, less than 5 percent of the campus population was black. You easily start to feel as though you are not wanted. You would experience subtle cues that just reinforced this feeling. A look here. A glance there. The stress of trying to fit in and to find your place fell on your shoulders quickly. That was the least of my worries though.

It would be an understatement to say that I was confused as I stared at my 2.2 GPA going into my second term of college. I was barely passing my introductory courses and on my way to flunking out. How did I get to this point? I still worried about my mother back home, but the hardest part was the coursework. When I was in high school, I could easily crank out an A on a test only after studying for an hour. A long essay was considered to be two pages. Now I was faced with having to write 6- to 10-page essays. I went to study sessions. I signed up for tutoring—anything I could do to increase my chances of getting a better grade. The better grades never came.

The stress of having to keep my image of the rising star full of potential and possibilities became too much. Stress led to anxiety. Anxiety led to depression. Everything started crumbling beneath me. I was becoming the disappointment I fought so hard not to become. I was letting everyone down.

Along with my internal struggles, I was also facing the stress of being a minority on campus. When you walk into a classroom where you are the only person of color, everyone including the instructor notices you. And they notice when you are not there. I hesitated to participate in class because I felt my responses would be stupid and then I would just be confirming stereotypes of black men. Or if the instructor wanted the opinion of what black individuals thought, I would feel the pressure of representing my race in class because I was the only person of color.

Seeing how all this was affecting me, a close friend of mine suggested that I talk to someone.

It was my first visit with my counselor which changed my perspective. She quickly pointed out that I was trying to solve an unsolvable problem. All the while I convinced myself that I could be trying harder when in fact I was trying too hard—trying to be someone I was not. It became clear to me that I no longer had to be the person people thought I should be in high school. I did not have to get an A on every exam or in every course. It felt like a huge source of stress had finally been lifted.

I pushed myself to talk with peers and joined other organizations for additional support. I met some great people who went through similar situations when they first came to college. Just knowing I was not alone in my experience and having advice on how to navigate my first year was a huge help. Eventually, I found my place. Spend some time to get to know who you are. Sometimes you just have to throw out old expectations and develop new ones for yourself.

WHAT IS SELF-CARE?

There is no question that college experience can be fun and exciting. Being in a different environment, meeting new people, and pursuing your dreams are positive aspects of entering college. However, college experience can also be challenging at times. Being away from home, trying to do well in classes, and getting along with a roommate can create stress. As you deal with the reality that college is stressful and challenging at times, you are faced with an important question: So what can I do about it? There is hope, and the answer rests with a few words: self-care. This chapter will help you gain a better understanding of what self-care is and why it is critical as you begin your college experience.

3.1: What It Is vs. What It Is Not

When you think of *self-care*, what comes to mind? What does it mean to care for yourself? At the heart of self-care is a focus on tending to the needs of your mind, body, and for some individuals, your spirit. But what does that really mean? Let's break down the meaning of "care" a bit more.

Care as a noun means "the provision of what is necessary for the health, welfare, maintenance, and protection of someone or something" or "serious attention or consideration applied to doing something correctly or to avoid damage or risk." What stands out to you with both of those definitions? When we apply those definitions to ourselves, we see that self-care involves doing what is necessary to improve, maintain, and protect our health. You will inevitably have challenging moments in college, and self-care can help boost your well-being. You may feel like you are on an even keel and self-care can help you stay at that desired level. Finally, we have talked about the stressful moments that are guaranteed to be headed your way. While you do not have a crystal ball to see what those moments will be and when they will occur, self-care can help soften the blow when it arrives.

Now, let's look at the definition of care as a verb. To care means to "feel concern or interest or attach importance to something" or to "look after and provide for the needs of." Again, what stands out to you in those definitions? You may have noticed that self-care is not just something you do for yourself. Rather, it is an attitude you can have toward yourself. It is an attitude of intentionality, meaning that there is a purpose to your actions. For example, you don't listen to music to just listen to "something." Rather, you purposefully listen to music to clear your mind when you have a difficult day. It is a way for you to decompress and deal with your internal struggles. This action is called "self-care."

So what is the purpose exactly? Well, you might just say self-care, right? While this might be true, it is important to introduce a new term that is similar to self-care—*wellness*. While taking care of yourself does serve a purpose, it leads to a greater goal of achieving wellness. So what is wellness exactly and how does it relate to self-care? Wellness is defined as "a way of life oriented toward optimal health and well-being, in which body, mind, and spirit are integrated by the individual to live life more fully within the human and natural community. Ideally, it is the optimum state of health and well-being that each individual is capable of achieving." Phew! That is a long definition. Let's break it down.

The first part of the definition states that wellness is focused on optimal health and well-being. This means that you are going about your days as best as you possibly can. And this differs for each person. The important point is to ask yourself, "Am I functioning as best as I possibly can?"

The second piece of the definition highlights that wellness involves attending to not just your body, but to your mind and your spirit as well. This means that wellness takes on a more holistic approach—meaning that all parts interact with one another. As you will learn in the next chapters, you will see a connection between all the different parts of yourself. As you attend to one part, it will affect others. So your mind, body, and spirit are all interconnected. Wellness involves an understanding of these interconnections. The goal is to achieve balance between these interconnections.

To give you a visual depiction of how wellness involves many different environmental and biological factors which are interconnected between your mind, body, and spirit, we have included the *Wheel of Wellness*. This model was the first of its kind to identify the multiple connections that impact your overall health and longevity. Take a look at the wheel and notice what

Figure 3.1

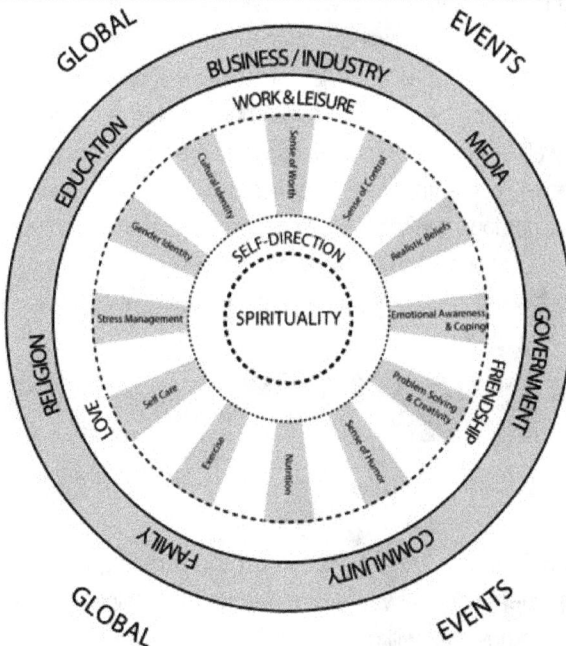

stands out to you. There are a few points which we will highlight. You will notice that spirituality is at the center indicating that it is the most important characteristic of your well-being. We devote an entire chapter at the end of the book to spirituality. For now, we will mention that spirituality refers to having a sense of meaning and purpose in life.

You will notice 12 spokes in the wheel that promote a sense of self-direction. These spokes aim to direct you in a positive direction as you respond to demands of work and leisure activities, developing friendships, and having romantic relationships. On the outside of the wheel, you will see different forces in life such as media and government that affect your wellness. Finally, this model highlights that all the components are interactive. So as you make adjustments to one area, changes will be experienced in other areas.

You must learn how to live and interact with the world around you. It would be great if we could all live healthy, happy lives in a little bubble and not have to deal with others, right? Wrong! Part of living in this world means dealing with your natural surroundings. We can discourage ourselves when we are afraid to meet the tasks that life presents. This discouragement usually takes the form of avoidance. When we avoid what is uncomfortable, we tend to engage in unhealthy and self-destructive behaviors. You will come to understand that to achieve your wellness goals you will most likely have to involve other people. Acknowledging and embracing this interdependence with others will be key to your welfare and success in college.

The final piece of the definition talks about achieving a state of *optimum* health and well-being, which means that you achieve the best or most favorable state possible. It is important to remember that your optimum health and well-being might look very different from someone else's. Your physical optimum might be running 10 miles, while someone else can only run 3 miles. As you engage in self-care, you will see that it is more about quality than quantity.

YOUR TURN 3.1

Where I am vs. Where I want to be

Directions: Take some time to reflect on the following prompts and rate yourself on where you feel you are currently. Then, think about where you want to be and how you will get there.

1. I would rate my current physical condition as a _____.

1	2	3	4	5	6	7	8	9	10
Very Poor	Poor			Okay		Good			Excellent

2. I would ideally like it to be a _____.

1	2	3	4	5	6	7	8	9	10
Very Poor	Poor			Okay		Good			Excellent

3. I would rate my current state of mental health as a _____.

1	2	3	4	5	6	7	8	9	10
Very Poor	Poor			Okay		Good			Excellent

4. I would ideally like it to be a _____.

1	2	3	4	5	6	7	8	9	10
Very Poor	Poor			Okay		Good			Excellent

5. I would rate my connection to the world around me as a _____.

1	2	3	4	5	6	7	8	9	10
Very Poor	Poor			Okay		Good			Excellent

6. I would ideally like it to be a _____.

1	2	3	4	5	6	7	8	9	10
Very Poor	Poor			Okay		Good			Excellent

Tool Box 3.1

- Self-care is about improving, maintaining, or protecting your health.
- Self-care is an attitude of intentionality.
- Wellness involves the optimal functioning of your mind, body, and spirit which leads to greater life satisfaction, meaning, and purpose.

Did You Know?

- Traditional college students (ages 18–23) perceive physical behaviors to be most important to their overall wellness including emotional, social, occupational, intellectual, and spiritual aspects.
- Nontraditional college students (ages 24 and older) perceive social activities as the most important factor.
- Nontraditional college students are more likely to engage in self-care practices than traditional college students because life experiences prove that self-care is important and risky behaviors are unhealthy and can lead to negative events in life.

3.1: Guilt for Practicing Self-Care

One of the first hurdles with practicing self-care is getting over the myth that self-care is a selfish act. Overcoming this feeling can be very difficult since taking care of oneself typically brings guilt to people. All our lives we are told that we should be there for others—that it is our responsibility to put others before ourselves. When we try to take of ourselves, we may be told or made to feel that we have been selfish. For example, your friends may want you to listen to their problems, but you have to study for the final exam. You may experience feelings of guilt because you feel like you somehow let them down when they need you. So when the next opportunity arrives to engage in self-care, we remember these feelings of guilt which override our logic. The end result is we forget the importance of caring for ourselves. However, it is important to keep in mind that you have to be well before trying to help others.

Our culture seems preoccupied with constantly staying busy whether that is to earn money so you can put food on the table, study a lot so you get good grades, go to class so you can earn your degree, or work hard so you can land that next promotion. When you wake up in the morning, do you ever consider what you are going to do that day to take care of yourself? Probably not! You are most likely thinking about how you will have enough time to get everything done that you need to accomplish for the day. What is the saying? "Work now—play later," right? The point is that we have created a culture that puts self-care at the bottom of the list. We have also taught ourselves that to practice self-care is an act of selfishness and we could be doing "better" things with our time. We also seem to have this belief that we can just keep giving and serving others without any repercussions. We do not seem to realize that our energy is limited.

Do not misunderstand—it is a wonderful trait if you enjoy doing things for others and taking care of those around you. However, if you do not learn to take care of yourself, you put your mind and body at risk for additional harm. Without self-care, you will lose energy. If you do not stop to take the time to refuel, you will find yourself constantly struggling and running on empty. Consequently, you may experience feelings of resentment and feeling like a burden to others. Most importantly, those relationships you enjoy so much will begin to suffer. Remember the following saying: "You cannot give what you do not have."

YOUR TURN 3.2

Tending to My Mind, Body, and Spirit

Directions: Now that we have talked about self-care and wellness as focused on a mind–body–spirit connection, take a moment to reflect on how you have been tending to each aspect. Identify and list ways in which you have currently been either taking care of each piece or neglecting them.

I have been taking care of my body by:

_____

_____

_____

I have been neglecting my body by:

_____

_____

_____

I have been taking care of my mind by:

_____

_____

_____

I have been neglecting my mind by:

_____

_____

_____

I have been taking care of my spirit by:

_____

_____

_____

I have been neglecting my spirit by:

_____

_____

_____

Tool Box 3.2

- Sometimes we can feel guilt and selfishness for wanting to take time out to help ourselves.
- The energy we use to care for ourselves and others is finite.
- Lack of self-care can lead to negative health consequences such as burnout and resentment.

Did You Know?

- About two-thirds of college students engage in self-care practices before visiting a student health service center for symptoms that led to their visit.

- Popular sources of self-care information include family members or friends, previous encounters with a healthcare provider, or medication advertisements.

- College students most often cite their college's website as the primary source of mental health services and support. Helpful website tools include availability to make online appointments, completing online mental health screening, information on accessing accommodations and free mental health services, and a frequently asked questions page.

3.2: Recovery, Healing, and Self-Preservation

As we mentioned in the previous chapter, the next years of your life will present challenges that you probably do not realize are even possible at this point. It is essential that you accept these moments as being inevitable. Doing so will allow you to put more attention into being proactive and coming up with ways to take care of yourself when these moments arrive. We want to drive this point home to you because this book is not designed to stop unfortunate events from occurring. Rather, this book is designed to educate you on how self-care can be a critical component of your success in college and beyond.

A simple analogy that resembles the concepts in this chapter is when you become sick. You cannot predict when or how you will get sick, but the odds are high that you will become ill at some point in your life. Sure there are things you can do to lessen your chances of getting sick like washing your hands. And if by chance you do get a cold, you have options available to help ease the symptoms. You still have to ride out the illness, but you do not have to feel as miserable. By using this analogy, you can see how self-care and wellness is focused on recovery and healing.

Odds are you will be faced with difficult circumstances in college that test your mind and body. You can take proactive steps to prevent situations from occurring or becoming out of control. If a situation does occur, you can engage in activities to help ease the stress and suffering. They can be anything that helps you feel centered and recharges your battery. This is where self-preservation comes in.

Remember that self-care is not self-centeredness—it is self-compassion. Making an effort to love yourself will help you grow, heal, and become more resilient to the stress and obstacles that you will face in college. So take these small steps toward loving yourself. Listen to your mind and body when it is sending signals to you that it is in distress, needs to relax, or needs to be more active. This may sound cliché but as you put the concepts in this book into practice, give yourself a pat on the back each moment you practice self-care. Acknowledge the effort you put into loving and caring for yourself. These small actions will help reinforce why you are engaging in wellness. Having a strong wellness routine will make your college experience that much more enjoyable and rewarding. So let's get started!

YOUR TURN 3.3 HOW DO I CARE FOR MYSELF?

Directions: Take some time now to review how you currently heal and recover from challenging situations.

1. Overall, how much time and effort do I put into caring for myself?

2. When I become physically sick, how do I care for my body?

3. When I am feeling anxious or depressed, how do I care for and tend to my mind and thoughts?

_____

_____

_____

4. When stressful events occur in my life, what do I do to get myself through these moments?

_____

_____

_____

Tool Box 3.3

- Self-care and wellness is about healing, recovering, and preserving your self during difficult life experiences.
- Self-care is an act of self-love.
- Self-care will lead to a more rewarding and enjoyable college experience.

Did You Know?

- Most college students report their general health to be excellent, very good, or good.
- Health issues such as stress management, sleep, and anxiety are reported to negatively impact first-year college students.
- First-year college students often report struggling with nutrition as they transition to a more independent lifestyle.

Surviving

How do you learn to care for yourself when all you have known your entire life is taking care of others? When I look back on my childhood, if I can even say it was a childhood, I always had to care for my family. I basically had to learn how to be an adult by the age of 10. My father had early onset Alzheimer's disease and my mother struggled with both diabetes and breast cancer. It fell on me to take care of the cooking and day-to-day chores around the house. I was up at 4 a.m. prepping meals and organizing medications only to spend the rest of the day at school worrying about whether they took their medications correctly or whether there was an accident or crisis waiting for me when I got off the school bus. When I was old enough to drive, I was the one taking my parents to a seemingly endless number of doctor appointments and emergency room visits. I wish I could erase all the memories of countless hours spent on the phone arguing with insurance companies over medical bills.

It was almost impossible for me to think about having a single moment to myself. As I look back, it feels as though my entire youth was spent monitoring, checking, resolving, or preventing one problematic situation after the other. My life felt as though it was always in the future—there was no time to worry about the past, and the present moments could be used to take care of the unknown to come.

When my father passed away, I was going into my senior year of high school. During the first half of the school year, my mom's health quickly spiraled downhill. I think the loss of my dad was just too much for her on top of the illnesses she was battling. With my dad being gone, it gave me some more free time to spend with my mother. I am grateful for the last few months I had with her because it was the closest we had ever been our entire lives. I talked to her about my fears of going on alone, and she told me her regrets of not being a better mother and letting me enjoy my childhood. But she made me promise her that I would move on and go to college. She died the day after my high school graduation.

I still remember that summer before I left for college. I remember it for one particular reason—the silence. Before my parents died, there was always some sort of noise going on—either one of them yelling for me to help them with something, the sound of my father walking around late at night, or the endless noise of the television which my mother spent the last half of her life in front of. Now, there was just silence. It almost seemed deafening. And with the silence came an awkward and uncomfortable feeling—a feeling of stillness. I was used to being busy and occupied with taking care of my parents. Now that I had nothing to do, it was like I had no more sense of purpose. Just an irritating question that kept nagging at me like a splinter in my mind—"Now what do I do?"

I worked a couple summer jobs to make the time pass by. Eventually, the day came when I packed what little I had and left for college. I decided to attend out of state so it would give me a fresh start. I figured a new environment would be good for me and I could leave home behind me.

I remember the first semester being incredibly stressful, and I had a difficult time adjusting. You would think that being so organized and on top of things with my parents would be a strength going into college, but you would be wrong. My life became unmanageable. I remember feeling so ashamed and embarrassed. I wondered how I could let things fall apart this way when I was able to do everything for my parents. One of my instructors noticed that I was having difficulties in my class and suggested that I talk with a counselor.

Although I was reluctant to go, it was one of the most rewarding experiences I have had in my life. It took me some time to become comfortable and trust him, but my counselor was incredibly kind and supportive from beginning to end. He helped me realize that I was more lost than ever because I never learned how to take care of myself. Through our talks together, he helped me realize that my struggles were normal and that there was hope. We spent the first year working on various issues. He helped me work through the grief of my parents' death and the loss of my own childhood, while also figuring out my next steps forward. He helped me learn to turn the care that I gave to my parents onto myself. Looking back on it, my counselor helped me get to know me. Our talks about self-care and wellness opened up opportunities for me that I never thought were possible. I no longer felt like I was just surviving—I was finally living.

Image Credit

- Fig. 3.1: Copyright © 1996 by Jane Myers, Thomas Sweeney, and Melvin Witmer.

TAKING CARE OF YOUR BODY

D o you ever find yourself super exhausted and feeling like you have emptied all of your energy? Do you ever feel like you can't even open your eyes after a sleepless night? It is almost certain that, at some point, you experience these feelings. In this chapter, you learn about ways to take care of your body so it takes care of you. It is important to remember that each topic discussed in this chapter is a significant component in helping you maintain a healthy lifestyle including diet, exercise, sleep, and more! No topic is more important than the other. Make sure you are engaging in each of the activities so that you will have a better idea of how you can be taking better care of yourself.

4.1: Sleep

Sleep is one of your most basic yet essential biological functions. Sleep is a natural part of your body's daily cycle and is an essential function in living a healthy life. It is just as important as other daily activities such as your diet and exercise. You spend almost one-third of your life sleeping. Seriously, think about that for a second! At least 30 percent of your life is spent asleep. That should highlight just how important it is for you to be maintaining a regular and healthy sleep schedule.

Did You Know?

- Humans are the only mammals that willingly delay sleep.
- Most adults need around seven to nine hours of sleep a night.
- You naturally feel tired around 2:00 a.m. and 2:00 p.m. This is one of the reasons why you feel you need that nap after lunch!
- Typically, it should take you 10 to 15 minutes to fall asleep.

YOUR TURN 4.1

Sleep Assessment

Directions: Take some time to reflect on the following questions about your sleep patterns.

1. In the past month, I usually went to bed at _____ a.m./p.m.

2. It usually takes me _____ hours/minutes to fall asleep.

3. In the past month, I usually woke up at _____ a.m./p.m.

4. On average, I probably get about _____ hours of sleep each night.

It is helpful to understand the reality of how the college experience will affect your ability to achieve enough sleep to function on a daily basis. Sleep problems can be influenced by negative (e.g., stress) and positive (e.g., excitement) situations. As you progress throughout your college years, your sleep problems, if they develop, may likely worsen. This should not be too surprising. During your first few years in college, you are trying to balance all the responsibilities of being in college and becoming an adult. Let's be honest—if your parents are no longer enforcing when you should be going to bed, you are probably going to want to stay up later watching TV or playing video games. It is also tempting to not want to go to class in the morning as well.

There are a number of other reasons why sleep may be affected during your first years in college. You may sign up for specific activities that, although fun and enriching, take time away from getting more sleep. You may already have health problems that interfere with your ability to sleep. Chances are you will be making new friends and interacting with people on a daily basis, and social expectations or pressures to go to parties or to stay out later may get in the way of sleeping well. You may also experience higher levels of stress due to the demands of your classes and job (if you are working).

Did You Know?

- 25 percent to 50 percent of college students report significant levels of daytime sleepiness.
- 67 percent of adolescents who had sleep problems were more likely to develop mental health problems during college.
- Students who had higher grades in college reported that they went to bed and woke up earlier than peers with lower grades
- 50 percent of students report difficulty sleeping, going to bed later, and not sleeping as much as they would ideally like to sleep.

YOUR TURN 4.2

Assessing for Sleep Disturbances

Directions: Review the list below and put a checkmark next to each item you have experienced in the last 30 days. This can give you an idea of whether you may be experiencing problems with your sleep. If you find yourself experiencing more than three of these problems in the past 30 days and they begin to interfere with your daily functioning (e.g., studying, working), it may be wise to seek out professional help such as individual counseling to explore more about these issues.

_____ It takes over 30 minutes to fall asleep.

_____ I wake up in the middle of the night or early morning.

_____ I have to get up and use the bathroom frequently.

_____ I have difficulties breathing, coughing, or snoring loudly.

_____ I experience frequent bad dreams or nightmares.

_____ I experience pain in my body.

_____ I have to take prescription or over-the-counter medications to help me sleep.

_____ I have problems staying awake when I drive, while eating, or when I am socializing with friends or family.

_____ I have little motivation to study, finish assignments, or accomplish other daily tasks.

Sleep problems can be classified in a number of different ways. For example, you may have difficulty falling asleep at night. Other common problems include staying asleep and waking up early or waking up frequently during the night. Do you know that insomnia is often found to be a significant problem among college students? Around 4 percent to 14 percent of young adults (ages 19–24) experience insomnia. College students who have been diagnosed with insomnia also experience increased fatigue, depression, anxiety, and stress. These symptoms are by-products of sleeplessness. People suffering from insomnia are more likely to report a lower quality of life. Ironically, many college students may seek stimulants (e.g., coffee, energy drinks, smoking) to help keep them awake during the day. Around 60 percent of college students use stimulants so that they can manage through the day. The use of stimulants makes insomnia even worse! Approximately 11 percent of college students report using alcohol to help them fall asleep. That statistic is very alarming because the continued and unmonitored use of alcohol can place a person at risk of substance misuse.

To be diagnosed with insomnia, you have to meet specific criteria. Symptoms can include difficulty falling asleep, frequent awakenings, and difficulty returning to sleep. As always, if you have concerns, you should contact a medical or mental health professional to be assessed. It is important to seek treatment for insomnia if experiencing symptoms because it is linked to substance use, anxiety or mood disturbances, and suicide. Be proactive about your health. Remember that there are ways you can promote healthy sleeping habits. Toward the end of this chapter, there are some strategies you can use to promote a healthy lifestyle, including healthy sleep.

Unfortunately, when you start experiencing problems with sleep, you are going to start seeing additional problems in your overall mental health. Sometimes, a brief period of not getting much sleep can cause significant issues. You may start experiencing symptoms of anxiety, depression, or irritability. If you had ongoing sleep problems during high school, it is likely that the struggle will continue in college. You are also more likely to experience anxiety or depression as a result of your insomnia, especially if you do not seek professional help. Chances are you have already encountered difficulties concentrating during class because you did not get enough sleep the previous night. However, since you may be working while you are in college, this lack of sleep will start affecting your abilities at work as well. In some cases, you may become agitated and start acting out aggressively toward others. Not getting enough sleep can be dangerous and life threatening because you are at risk for causing traffic accidents.

There are significant advantages to maintaining a healthy sleep regimen. Achieving enough sleep can help you fight off illnesses by boosting your immune system. This is a good way to avoid getting sick from all of those germs on campus. When you are getting adequate sleep, you also have more focused concentration and your memory is sharpened. This means you are less likely to doze off during a lecture or forget a major quiz coming up. You also have more energy to engage in physical activities. A regular sleep schedule can also be critical in maintaining your emotional health.

There are many ways you can improve your sleep hygiene. First, try to exercise on a regular basis so you can release physical and mental stress from your body. Although it may difficult to find the time or get motivated to exercise, it is important that you do it to promote your physical and psychological health. Second, avoid drinking caffeine and using nicotine products. These products, otherwise known as stimulants, activate your system to make you more alert which is the exact opposite of what you want when you are trying to fall asleep. Allow your body to develop its natural rhythm for going to bed and waking up. Going against your natural sleep cycle only causes more stress. Also try to set some time out for daydreaming or meditation. This might sound odd, but it can help you relax and feel centered. This technique allows you to have the time to sit with your thoughts and empty them from your mind. Giving yourself this time will help you when you go to bed because you won't spend so much time dwelling on what is floating around in your mind or stressing you out. You will have already had that time to reflect and will fall asleep quicker. Last but not least, turn off your electronic devices! Results of many scientific studies confirm that people who have a hard time putting away that phone and tablet are at risk for developing sleep problems and, in fact, other health problems such as neck and wrist pain.

YOUR TURN 4.3

Improving My Sleep Hygiene

Directions: Below is a list from the National Sleep Foundation on ways to improve your overall sleep hygiene. Review the table below and see which areas you could improve on.

Activity	I need to work on this	I'm doing okay with this
Avoid napping during the day		
Avoid stimulants such as caffeine, nicotine, and alcohol too close to bedtime		
Exercise can promote good sleep		
Stay away from large meals close to bedtime		
Ensure adequate exposure to natural light		
Try to avoid emotionally upsetting conversations and activities before trying to go to sleep		
Associate your bed with sleep		
Make sure that the sleep environment is pleasant and relaxing		

Tool Box 4.1

- Sleep is critical to the daily functioning of your body.
- Not getting enough sleep can have serious impacts on your physical and emotional health.
- Maintaining good sleep hygiene can help you get the rest your body needs.

4.2: Exercise

Exercise is a natural way of taking care of and strengthening your body. Exercise helps improve your mind, body, and spirit. Exercise benefits people of all ages. In adolescents, exercise helps regulate hormones and promote physical development. No wonder you were asked to participate in physical education classes in middle and high school! In adults, exercise becomes a critical component in the body's ability to manage and recover from physical and psychological illnesses. However, finding the motivation and determination to stay active can be daunting. In fact, late adolescence is the period of time when you are least likely to be active in your life. To make matters worse, about 54 percent of adults do not meet guidelines of exercising at even a moderate level. It is safe to assume that you are most likely facing an uphill battle to begin with. Fortunately, there are ways to increase your level of motivation to exercise. The key is to make exercise a part of your daily routine. Here is how.

When you are thinking about exercising, it can be helpful to understand what your intentions are for exercising. Do I want to lose weight? Do I want to strengthen my body? Am I trying to condition my body for a specific sport? Do I notice myself having more energy and feeling better emotionally after I exercise? These intentions are a result of three important factors: your attitude towards working out, your level of motivation from encouragement by others such as peers or family, and your own perceptions about your ability to exercise.

YOUR TURN 4.4

Assessing My Physical Activity

Directions: Take a moment to reflect on and write out some responses to the following questions.

1. How has your level of physical activity changed throughout your life?

    _____

    _____

    _____

2. Describe your current attitude(s) toward physical activity and exercise.

    _____

    _____

    _____

3. How important are physical activity and exercise in your life?

    _____

    _____

    _____

4. What are some barriers that get in the way of you exercising?

    _____

    _____

    _____

5. Who do you have in your life that could encourage you to be physically active? In what ways could they encourage you?

    _____

    _____

    _____

You are most likely to fall into one of two categories when thinking about the reasons for exercising. The first category includes exercising for appearance-related purposes. This includes wanting to look physically attractive to others, maintaining a desired weight, or toning up your body. It should be noted that you are more likely to develop eating disorders or experience low self-esteem if your primary motivation for exercising is to look a certain way.

The other category includes exercising for nonappearance-related reasons. These could include experiencing enjoyment from exercising and socializing with others. Other reasons may include changing your mood if you are feeling anxious or depressed, feeling a sense of accomplishment, and trying to lose weight for health purposes. Most college students have reported nonappearance-related reasons as primary motivators for exercising. However, gender differences do play a role in what is a primary motivator for exercise among college students. For example, men are more likely to exercise due to a desire for health and physical attractiveness whereas women exercise to feel better emotionally and psychologically.

YOUR TURN 4.5

How I Feel About Exercising

Directions: Now that you have completed your own reflection, review the tables below and circle your own common attitudes, beliefs, and barriers towards exercising.

My Attitude Toward Exercising

1. Exercise is probably the best thing I can do for my health right now.
2. I agree that exercise is important for my health, but there are just other things that are more important to me right now.
3. I do not think that exercise is very important for my health.

Reasons Why I Do Not Exercise

1. I am afraid I may get hurt.
2. I am too tired or don't have enough energy.
3. I am under a lot of stress right now.
4. I can't afford a membership.
5. I do not have a place to walk.
6. I do not have anyone who would exercise with me.
7. I don't have enough time.
8. I feel self-conscious.
9. I feel too anxious.

10. I feel too depressed.

11. I have other health problems that might interfere.

12. I would have to learn too much.

13. My spouse or partner does not want me to exercise.

14. Weather.

Benefits of Exercising

1. I am able to spend time with family.

2. I can monitor my weight.

3. I do not get sick as much.

4. I feel I have more energy.

5. I feel that I have more control in my life.

6. I get to hang out with friends.

7. I have better sex.

8. I have higher self-esteem.

9. I have less stress.

10. I look better.

11. It helps me slow down the aging process.

12. It is just fun for me.

It doesn't matter why you choose to engage in exercise. Regular exercise can have numerous benefits to your ability to think and make decisions. Exercise helps excite your central nervous system. This helps you absorb sensory information more quickly and you also are able to block out information that is not really necessary. As a result, you become more focused and your short-term and long-term memory are increased. This can be helpful in not only remembering that you have an exam coming up but also helpful in recalling information for that exam!

Speaking of exams, exercise can be a great way to reduce study-related fatigue. This occurs when you become stressed out about your academic grades and are studying beyond what your body and mind can adapt to. Exercise can help distract you from all of the worry and anxiety about upcoming exams or assignments. You can become more relaxed, refreshed, and ready to tackle your assignments and studies with a clearer mind. Exercise is also a great way to lower your blood pressure, which increases from added stress and at elevated levels can have significant negative effects on your overall well-being.

Physical exercise can also be helpful in reducing your likelihood of experiencing depression. Given the significant adjustment to college life, you may struggle with meeting new people, keeping up with your academic assignments, or balancing your free time with other responsibilities. These all could lead you to feel depressed and hopeless. There have been numerous studies which show that regular exercise can reduce symptoms of depression and suicidal behaviors. It is important to try to remain active if you feel like you may be experiencing depression. We will talk about depression in more detail in a later chapter.

Did You Know?

- Regular exercise can decrease your risk of developing high blood pressure, high cholesterol, and heart disease.
- Walking is the simplest change you can make to improve your health.
- Exercising three to four times a week for about 40 minutes can result in significant positive changes to your overall physical and mental health.
- Only one-fifth of college students meet public health recommendations of exercising for 30 minutes a day for five or more days per week.

Keep in mind that there are many different ways that you can exercise. You do not have to visit the gym every day or do 300 push-ups. You can be creative and find outlets to get your body moving in ways that you personally enjoy. This can be done in the comfort of your own place or while getting out and exercising with your friends or family. And remember, the key is to make exercise a part of your daily routine so it becomes your habit.

YOUR TURN 4.6

My Preferred Physical Activities

Directions: Take a moment to review the list below and select the activities that appeal most to you. Put a checkmark next to each activity that you would enjoy doing. Remember to be realistic and honest with yourself. Use this as a guide for developing your own exercise activities and routine.

1. Aerobics
2. Biking
3. Climbing stairs
4. Dancing
5. Exercise bike
6. Gardening
7. Hiking
8. Housework
9. Job-related activities
10. Jogging
11. Push-ups
12. Running
13. Shopping
14. Stair machine
15. Stretches
16. Swimming
17. Taking care of children
18. Treadmill
19. Walking
20. Walking the dog
21. Water aerobics
22. Weight lifting
23. Yard work
24. Yoga

Exercise can also be beneficial if you are struggling with chronic pain. Regular exercise has been shown to help increase your tolerance to pain. You should also remember that pain is not just a sensation felt by neurons and receptors in your body but is also related to your emotions (e.g., fear of experiencing pain) and behaviors (e.g., avoiding activities that activate pain).

Tool Box 4.2

- Physical exercise can help your body stay stronger, live longer, and fight off or recover from illnesses.
- Just doing a minimum amount of exercise each day can lead to significant effects on your physical and psychological health.
- Examine your values and barriers toward exercise to help you remain motivated.

4.3: Nutrition

Insomnia is just one of the many negative consequences of a poor diet—a diet that may be high in sugars, fats, and sodium. Let's face it, you are less likely, as a first-year college student, to be consuming fruits, vegetables, and dairy products. There are so many parties and events on and off campus that you go to and they do not typically offer healthy food. If you are not staying physically active, you are more likely to become overweight and possibly obese. Unfortunately, trends toward an unhealthy lifestyle have only been increasing. Among college students, overweight and obesity trends have increased 11.9 percent from 1995 (20.5%) to 2011 (32.4%). These figures should not be all too surprising considering you are likely to spend about 40 percent of your food budget at fast-food or sit-down restaurants. This means you you prefer meals that are convenient and inexpensive.

Did You Know?

- Your typical diet probably exceeds recommended intake levels for solid fats and added sugars, refined grains, sodium, and saturated fat.
- Only 6.2 percent of college students consume the recommended five or more fruits and vegetables per day.
- 35 percent of college students report being overweight.
- Since the 1970s, the number of fast-food restaurants has more than doubled.

There are probably numerous reasons why you may find it difficult to maintain a healthy diet while in college. Many college students report that they do not have adequate access to healthy foods. Also, if you are coming from a home where your meals were prepared for you, then you are less likely to know how to prepare healthy meals or have the skills to do so. You are also likely to mimic the type of meals that were made for you as a child.

"But how do I know what is healthy or what I should be eating?" This is an important question. The Office of Disease Prevention and Health Promotion set out a list of dietary guidelines that can assist you in figuring out what you should be putting in your body and how much. We have included the information in the table below. The information below is based on a 2,000-calorie/day diet for an adult.

Food group/ingredients	Daily recommended amount
Vegetables	2.5 cups per day
Fruits	2 cups per day
Grains	6 ounces per day
Dairy	3 cups per day
Protein	5.5 ounces per day
Seafood	8 or more ounces per week
Meats and Poultry	26 ounces per week
Oils	5 teaspoons per day
Added sugars	Less than 10% of calories per day

Saturated fats	Less than 10% of calories per day
Sodium	Less than 2,300 mg per day
Alcohol	Up to 1 drink per day for women Up to 2 drinks per day for men
Caffeine	Up to 400/mg per day

YOUR TURN 4.7

Food Diary

Directions: Take a moment to fill out this food diary based on the last seven days. What do you notice about the information you put into the dairy? Does the information in your diary line up with the recommended guidelines set out by the 2015–2020 Dietary Guidelines for Americans by the Office of Disease Prevention and Health Promotion?

Meal	Day of the Week				
	Monday	Tuesday	Wednesday	Thursday	Friday
Breakfast					
Lunch					
Dinner					

Make sure you are checking in with your health and wellness centers on campus to see if they offer classes and activities for nutrition. This can be a great way to increase your knowledge and skills in preparing healthy meals. You can also be better prepared to combat the widely known "freshman 15." This term refers to the 15 pounds, on average, that many college students gain during their freshman year. This is mainly due to eating large portions of unhealthy foods and not exercising regularly on top of not getting enough sleep during the night and having low physical energy. As you can see, it is a vicious cycle!

It is important that you are controlling the amount of calories you eat and making sure you are exercising. One of the leading causes of obesity is a discrepancy in the amount of calories you are putting in your body versus the amount of exercise you are getting. If you ingest a lot of calories but do not engage in any physical activities to burn off those excess calories, your body will store those calories as fat. As a college student, you are at increased risk for weight gain and obesity because of unhealthy eating habits or not exercising regularly. Remember, weight gain can interfere not only with your physical and psychological health, but also your academic performance (i.e., not feeling good resulting in a lack of motivation and absences in class).

One of the reasons you are not eating healthy foods might be because you just do not have the knowledge to make informed choices. You may be looking at food labels but you also may be reading them incorrectly. So be sure to educate yourself on how to properly evaluate the information on food labels. You are more likely to select healthier foods as a result.

College life can be very busy—busy enough that you start skipping meals because you have to rush to class or get to work on time. College students often neglect eating breakfast out of all the meals in the day. Eating the recommended amount of meals each day can be helpful in reducing your chances of becoming overweight. Eating breakfast is essential to a healthy diet, but you should also be mindful of what you are eating for that meal.

Remember that earlier we discussed the importance of getting enough sleep? Well, turns out that there is an important relationship between you sleeping well and your diet. If you are not sleeping enough, this may affect certain metabolic hormones such as ghrelin and leptin. These hormones are key in regulating how hungry and satiated you feel. Researchers have also found that less sleep affects neurons in different brain regions that are responsible for executive functioning and mood. In other words, because you are not sleeping enough, you may be more inclined to sit on the couch longer and gorge on your favorite ice cream or potato chips.

Tool Box 4.3

- The number of students reporting poor diets and being over-weight has been increasing over the last decade.
- A poor diet can put you at greater risk for health-related complications in the future.
- Following recommended guidelines can ensure that you are getting the right foods and nutrients in your diet.

4.4: Chronic Conditions

Chronic conditions and disabilities can affect an individual in numerous ways. Each effect can have a direct impact on a person's physical and emotional well-being. Managing a chronic illness or disability can seem insurmountable at times, and the demands of college do not make it any easier. You may be juggling multiple doctor appointments, getting your prescriptions filled, taking your medications as prescribed, or handling any flare-ups with your condition. This is why it is important that you are informed of the many ways that you can seek assistance to improve your quality of life and the quality of your college experience. Doing so will help you prevent disruptions in your academics, increased health risks, and possibly dropping out of college.

Did You Know?

- 20 percent of young adults have a chronic medical condition.
- Most colleges do not have a system for identifying incoming students with chronic medical conditions.
- Under the Affordable Care Act, you can qualify for subsidized insurance or remain under your parent's insurance until the age of 26.

If you have a chronic condition or disability, you may have assumed that your options are limited when it comes to selecting a college or university to attend. Remember that you have certain protections and tools at your disposal under the law. For example, the Americans with Disabilities Act and Section 504 of the Rehabilitation Act provide services for individuals with disabilities and was set up to support you in achieving your highest potential in areas such as community life, employment, and self-sufficiency.

Your campus should have an accessibility resource center where you can request more information. If the college you are attending receives federal funding, they must ensure nondiscriminatory practices in the treatment of students with disabilities under Section 504 of the Rehabilitation Act. Remember that if you have a disability, you are entitled to accommodations that will enable you to participate fully on campus. Make sure you visit your campus disability resource center when you are attending orientation. You will have a chance to meet with and speak to staff who can address your questions and concerns regarding accommodations and how to go about receiving services.

Along with accommodations, the disability resource center may be able to provide counseling services. At times, individuals with a disability feel isolated and different. Group counseling can be beneficial in helping you connect with other students with similar issues so you feel less isolated and more support. It will also provide you an opportunity to speak about issues related to your college experience and living with a disability. Counseling can be a great resource, especially during your first year as you learn to adjust to the demands of college life.

One of the most common chronic conditions that adolescents and young adults face is type 1 diabetes. This condition is caused by your autoimmune system destroying its own insulin-producing cells. You may experience hypoglycemia which results in low blood sugar because your body cannot produce sufficient glucose. Common symptoms of hypoglycemia include shivering, sweating, tremors, blurred vision, dizziness, nausea, headaches, and muscle weakness. This is a serious condition and needs your immediate attention. If you do not manage the symptoms, you can be at higher risk for developing heart disease, stroke, and kidney damage.

Managing the symptoms of type 1 diabetes and keeping a healthy routine can take a considerable amount of time and effort. Unfortunately, college students often engage in risky behaviors such as drinking alcohol, poor diet, and sleep patterns that put these routines, and their subsequent health, at risk. You may be less likely to tell your friends or peers that you have type 1 diabetes for fear of rejection or discrimination from others. Although it is understandable that you want to fit in, taking risks with your health may not have immediate consequences but can certainly have long-term impacts as you get older.

Given the prevalence of type 1 diabetes among young adults such as yourself, it is important that you consult with a medical professional should you have any concerns about your health or symptoms you may be experiencing. Take advantage of your university health services and speak with professionals who can help you. They can also provide you with services or referral information so you can talk with a specialist. Managing your type 1 diabetes symptoms is the key to living a healthy and fulfilling life.

Tool Box 4.4

- Laws exist to help you gain access to resources so you can fully engage in your college experience.
- One of the most common chronic conditions is type 1 diabetes.
- Seek medical attention and resources to help manage symptoms of a chronic illness or disability.

4.5: Substance Use

Alcohol use is one of the biggest concerns for students on campus related to substance use. It remains the number one health issue on college campuses. More specifically, binge drinking is a common practice among college students. Binge drinking is defined as having four or more drinks in a row for women or five or more drinks in a row for men. You may have heard situations where excessive drinking leads to unpleasant (and often unthinkable) incidents, including sexual assault and other unwanted experiences. As a first-year student, you are more likely to experience alcohol dependence given the risks of transition from high school to college. You are also more likely at risk to abuse alcohol if your campus allows alcohol and you are not an athlete or member of a Greek organization.

Did You Know?

- Binge drinking accounts for more than 50 percent of alcohol consumed by adults.
- Binge drinking accounts for more than 90 percent of alcohol consumed by adolescents.
- Around 35–40 percent of students report abusing alcohol.
- Approximately 60–65 percent of college students have used alcohol in the past 30 days.

YOUR TURN 4.8

Assessing my Alcohol Use

Directions: Take a moment to answer the following questions about your own alcohol use.

1. I drink ...
   __ every day   __3–5 times a week   __once a week
   __only on weekends   __on special occasions
2. I drink five or more drinks in a sitting.
   __yes   __no
3. When I last socialized with others, I spent the following amount of time drinking ...
   __none   __one hour   __2–3 hours
   __4–5 hours   __more than five hours

4. When I last socialized, I had ...
   __ 0 drinks   __ 1–2 drinks   __ 3–4 drinks   __ 5–6 drinks
   __ 7–9 drinks   __ more than 9 drinks

5. In the last two weeks, I have had five or more drinks in one sitting ...
   __ 0 days   __1–2 days   __3–4 days   __5–6 days
   __every day

Often, students will report that they are drinking or using drugs to cope with stress, which is not surprising given all the demands that college places on you. Marijuana and alcohol can be used by students as a means to self-medicate, relax, and reduce stress. It would also make sense that if you found this method of coping to be effective, you would be less likely to try other coping strategies, even if they are safer and healthier.

Other reasons for engaging in alcohol use include social pressures from peers. Your closest friends and peers are likely to have the most influence over you. If they are drinking, you may feel the pressure to fit in with them to be accepted or respected. You want to feel like you belong to the group and to be included in activities, even if it means you will need to drink when you don't want to. You may have a hard time saying "NO" to your friends and roommates. Whatever the reason, you need to understand that it is important that you feel safe and make a thoughtful rather than impulsive decision when engaging in alcohol use. You may also think that your friends and peers are drinking more than you. This false overestimation may make you want to drink more just to keep up with them. Keep in mind that your perceptions about how much and how often people are drinking may not be accurate.

YOUR TURN 4.9

Pressures to Drink

Directions: Take a moment to reflect on and respond to the following questions.

1. How often do you feel pressured to drink or use drugs?

   _____

   _____

   _____

2. Where do those pressures come from?

   _____

   _____

   _____

3. How do you respond to those pressures? Do you end up using drugs or alcohol or do you stop yourself from using?

   _____

   _____

   _____

4. What are the outcomes of deciding to use or not use? What do you notice about yourself, your health, and the people around you?

   _____

   _____

   _____

The more you decide to drink or use drugs, the greater your chances of encountering devastating consequences to your health and future. These consequences may include getting into motor vehicle accidents, being the victim or perpetrator of physical or sexual violence, contracting a sexually transmitted disease (STD), or experiencing an unwanted or unplanned pregnancy. It is estimated that approximately 1,700 college students die per year from unintentional alcohol-related injuries such as motor vehicle accidents.

Review the list below and identify common physical consequences of your drug or alcohol use:

Physical Consequences	(past/present)
Headaches	/
Nausea	/
Nosebleeds	/
Tolerance	/
Sweating	/
Increased appetite	/
Fatigue	/
Vomiting	/
Using to avoid withdrawal symptoms	/
Rapid pulse rate	/
Decreased heart rate	/
Chronic cough	/
Hand tremors	/
Insomnia	/
Hypersomnia	/
Hangovers	/
Blackouts	/
Passing out/stupor	/
Psychomotor agitation	/
Seizures	/
Muscle aches	/
Muscle weakness	/
Lacrimation/rhinorrhea	/
Diarrhea	/
Yawning	/
Fever	/

Along with physical effects to your health and well-being, alcohol abuse can have serious consequences on your emotional and psychological health. You are more likely to experience high levels of depression as a result of alcohol abuse. This also puts you at risk for considering suicide or self-harming behaviors.

Review the list below and identify common psychological consequences of your drug or alcohol use:

Psychological Symptoms	(past/present)
Concentration difficulties	/
Memory loss/lapses	/
Disorganized thinking	/
Hallucinations	/
Bad dreams	/
Flashbacks	/
Irritability	/
Anxiety	/
Restlessness	/
Low mood	/
Depression	/
Mood changes	/
Sedation	/
Suicidal thoughts	/
Suicidal gestures	/
Anger	/
Paranoia	/
Homicidal thoughts	/
Violent behaviors	/
Inability to care for self	/

Persistent alcohol or drug abuse puts you at risk for developing a substance use disorder. The list below represents the symptoms found in substance use disorders. Review the list so you become more aware of the warning signs and symptoms.

1. The substance is often taken in larger amounts or over a longer period than was intended.

2. There is a persistent desire or unsuccessful efforts to cut down or control the substance use.
3. I spend a great deal of time in activities necessary to obtain, use, or recover from the effects of drugs or alcohol.
4. I notice cravings, strong desires, or urges to use drugs or alcohol.
5. Recurrent drug or alcohol use results in a failure to fulfill my obligations at work, school, or home.
6. I continue to use drugs or alcohol despite social or interpersonal problems caused by using drugs or alcohol.
7. I use drugs or alcohol in situations where it is physically hazardous such as driving.
8. I continue to use drugs or alcohol despite knowing that they are causing physical or psychological problems.
9. I have developed a tolerance to the drug or alcohol and need increased amounts to achieve the desired effect.
10. I experience withdrawal symptoms when not using alcohol or drugs.

In addition to life-threatening consequences, students will more frequently experience poorer academic performance as a result of drinking and drug use. If you binged on alcohol the previous night, the odds are high that you are more likely to miss class the next morning due to being hung over. Keep this behavior going and you put yourself at risk for falling behind in your classes, receiving poor grades, failing classes, and possibly dropping out. As you may expect, poor academic performance influences your future career decisions and potential as it may limit your opportunity to thrive in the world of work.

If you believe that you are struggling with alcohol or drug use, you need to seek professional help immediately. Remember that your struggle is real and you don't have to fight alone. Check with your campus health and counseling clinics to see what services are available. Counseling can help you identify triggers to your drug or alcohol use along with developing skills to reduce the frequency and duration of your use. Talking with a counselor can also help you work through underlying issues that may be tied to your substance use. Prescription medications are also available to assist in managing symptoms or cravings of drugs or alcohol.

Tool Box 4.5

- Alcohol abuse is a serious problem facing many college campuses.
- Continued alcohol abuse can have detrimental impacts on your health, ability to work, do well in school, and maintain healthy relationships.
- College campuses should have available resources and referral options if you are seeking help to manage drug or alcohol use.

VOICES FROM CAMPUS 4.1

A New Start

Sometimes, you really never know what you have until it is gone. I started my freshman year optimistically. I was on a full scholarship in law school. My girlfriend (the love of my life) and I were lucky enough to attend the same college. I also had a part-time job at a prestigious law firm with promises for advancement as I completed my degree and eventually graduated. Everything seemed perfect.

I had never been much of a drinker in high school. Sure my girlfriend and I would go to parties and had our drunken stupors a few times. But it was never anything serious or something I cared about. I had other priorities in my life, and my parents were pushing me to do well in school and to get into a high-ranking college.

I did not really know anyone at my new college so I went out to parties to meet new people and decompress after long days of classes and studying. Having a few drinks took the edge off a long day and made me more relaxed and less anxious when meeting new people. I started making friends and we would plan to hang out at other parties and events more frequently. But more parties led to more drinking and they kept on going.

Eventually, instead of a beer or two I was drinking four-plus beers plus hard liquor and this was just on weeknights. I would be so hung over that I was beginning to skip classes. My girlfriend started getting belligerent calls from me at 2 a.m. She would have to come get me because I was too drunk to drive home. She started worrying, and that worry turned into more fights between the two of us. This just made me want to drink even more. I started missing work—grades kept falling but I had it in the back of my mind that I could recover and nothing really bad would happen. Then the phone call came.

My supervisor at the law firm called me in for a meeting. I walked in to see that it was just not her—the heads of the firm were present along with a face I recognized as I passed by the HR department. I knew what was about to happen. They talked about my absenteeism and how the quality of my work had suffered, which led to a few embarrassing moments for the firm. They expressed their disappointment and how they had high hopes for me. In the end, they did not want to take any more risks with me. I had the career of a lifetime in the making—now it was gone.

My girlfriend was upset at first but then was supportive. She told me I needed to make a choice—the alcohol or her. I told her I would stop but I still went out. Eventually, we were not even fighting anymore—we just stopped talking. We grew apart and became like roommates. Then, the letter came.

Academic services sent a letter stating that my scholarship would not be renewed due to the decline in my grades. I was devastated again and became furious. I slammed the letter on the kitchen counter and went out to drink. I don't remember much except coming home the next morning to an empty apartment. There was a note from my girlfriend next to the letter from academic services. The note was short and to the point—"I'm done." That sinking feeling in the pit of my stomach hit again. I had the partner any guy would dream of having—now she was gone.

So here I was—alone, no job, feeling like a failure, and now having to tell my parents my scholarship was gone. It is amazing what can happen in almost a year's time and how your life can change. I went home to tell my parents and they were surprisingly supportive, but they gave me an ultimatum—treatment or I'm on my own. It was an easy decision—easy because I was terrified knowing that I had only one thing left to lose: my life.

I went to the campus support services and was connected with any and every service that could help support my recovery. I went to a counselor a few times a week and she really helped me understand my drinking, how to manage it, as well as talk about other personal issues that I think caused me to drink more. I went to other support groups that helped me connect with other students who were struggling with similar issues related to alcohol or drug use. It really helped me feel like I was not alone and gave me different perspectives.

Eventually, life became more manageable and things began falling back into place. I started taking more classes and avoiding situations where there was drinking. I kept busy by working part-time jobs and doing things I really enjoyed that were healthier and more fulfilling for me.

My advice to those of you who are reading this is to be responsible when you go out and drink. Don't get caught up in the thrill, excitement, or amusement of drinking. If my story is any example, it can have devastating consequences. And if you do find yourself having problems, go get help right away. Don't wait. There are great professionals and resources out there. You do not want to feel this sense of regret—trust me. I have been given another chance to build a great life for myself—and now I am going to take it.

TAKING CARE OF YOUR SEXUALITY

I n this chapter, we review how sexual health plays a major role in your overall wellness and life satisfaction. We review the basics of sexual health and how to engage in safe and healthy sexual practices. We also discuss intimate partner violence and how it may affect your relationships. Finally, we discuss issues surrounding nonconsensual sexual interactions and sexual assault and steps you can take to prevent or report its occurrence.

5.1: Sexual Health

College is a time for making lots of decisions. These include decisions about your sexuality and sexual health. Sexual health is defined by the World Health Organization as "a state of physical, mental and social well-being in relation to sexuality. It requires a positive and respectful approach to sexuality and sexual relationships, as well as the possibility of having pleasurable and safe sexual experiences, free of coercion, discrimination and violence." Decisions may include whether you want to abstain from having sex or become sexually active. You may also make decisions concerning the gender of your sexual partners and the type of protection and contraception to use.

Unfortunately, students enter college with little to no information regarding sexual health. Your reproductive and sexual health plays an important role in your overall health and well-being. Why? Because your sexual health can be tied to numerous unintended health outcomes such as pregnancy, human immunodeficiency virus (HIV), other sexually transmitted diseases (STDs), intimate partner violence, or sexual assault. Having more information and utilizing resources will help you make informed decisions which will lead to safer sex behaviors and reduce STD transmission.

Having a conversation regarding sexual health and practice can be difficult. It is important that you have trusted people you can talk to about sex. If you have questions about sex, consider talking with a counselor, trusted adult, or your parent(s)/guardian(s). You should also have a primary care provider or healthcare provider that you feel safe and comfortable sharing personal information. Talking with a health care provider can ensure that your conversations and information are kept confidential. A competent health care provider will answer all your questions and take the time to listen to any concerns and explain information so you understand.

Did You Know?

- Teenagers and young adults (ages 15–24) account for nearly 50 percent of all new STDs.
- 20- to 24-year-olds are more likely to experience an unintended pregnancy.
- STDs rates are twice as common among young adults (ages 20–24).

YOUR TURN 5.1

Assessing my Sexual Health Knowledge

Directions: Take some time to reflect on the following situations and questions regarding your sexual health.

1. What is my sexual orientation—my emotional and sexual attraction to others? (lesbian, gay, straight, bisexual, other, or don't know)

   _____

2. I want to make sure that my partner and I get tested before we have sex. Do I know where to go? What questions should I ask my doctor?

   _____

   _____

   _____

3. Do I have any desire to have (more) children?

   _____

4. What screenings are recommended for someone my age?

   _____

   _____

5. How can I talk to my partner about sex and STDs?

   _____

   _____

   _____

6. What are my options when it comes to birth control? How should I talk to my partner about these options?

   _____

_____

_____

For some of you, other areas influence your sexuality and sexual practice. Maybe it is your family tradition or religion not to talk about sex. Maybe it never occurs to you that you are not sure about the concept of an unwanted sexual experience. Whatever the reasons are, it is important for you to understand that sexual health is one of the most important life areas and you can benefit from discussing this with professionals. It is crucial that you attend to your sexual health and practice as it will have lifelong effects on your sexual experience. In many cultures and groups, one-night stands or sudden sexual engagement are common practice. However, these types of engagement also pose some risks to one's sexual health. If you are sexually active or decide to become sexually active, what are some things you should take into consideration? Well, it is important to have communication with your partner. Then you can decide whether you want to follow through with a sexual relationship. Part of this conversation should include asking about their sexual history and if they have been exposed to any STD. You can also request your partner get tested for STDs before having sex. Frequent testing on your part is also important.

Remember that the only way to guarantee that you will not acquire an STD is to abstain from sex. However, if you are sexually active, then the best way to avoid an STD is to have a sexual relationship with only one partner who has been tested and is negative for any communicable diseases. You should also use a latex condom each time you decide to have sexual inter-course. If you are going to have sexual relationships with multiple partners, then your chances of acquiring an STD increase and this requires you to closely monitor your sexual health.

If you need additional information and guidance, you can seek help from qualified professionals who can discuss with you the pros and cons as well as options. As a college student, you can visit your student health center; it is usually free of charge. Members of every gender can discuss options for practicing safe sex. You can talk about concerns you have in engaging in sexual interactions. For women, the center may offer birth control at a reduced cost or discuss options regarding unplanned or planned pregnancy.

YOUR TURN 5.2

My Thoughts Towards Sex

Directions: Reflect on the following questions regarding your decision to have a sexual relationship.

1. Am I able to talk with my partner about sex and their sexual history? Do I feel comfortable when I have these conversations?

   _____

   _____

2. Have I felt pressured into having sex with my partner? Is this decision my own?

   _____

   _____

3. Will my partner respect my decision not to have sex? How will they respond to my decision?

   _____

   _____

4. Have my partner and I talked about what would happen if I/they became pregnant or got an STD?

   _____

   _____

Tool Box 5.1

- Sexual health involves the attitudes, beliefs, and behaviors you engage in regarding your sexuality and sexual relationships.

- Often, college students have little knowledge about safe and healthy practices regarding their sexual health.

- Utilize resources such as your student health center or a primary care physician to stay informed of best practices regarding your sexual health.

- Best practices can help you avoid negative life outcomes.

5.2: Intimate Partner Violence

Intimate partner violence (IPV) is defined as violence that occurs in present or past intimate relationships. This violence can take different forms and produce negative relational outcomes. For example, the violence or harm can be psychological (e.g., emotional abuse), physical (e.g., hitting), or sexual (e.g., rape) in nature. These behaviors are used to gain power and control over a partner.

Numerous factors contribute to IPV. Depending on your gender, you may have a different attitude toward IPV. These are known as gender-role attitudes, which are attitudes that you learn are appropriate to your gender. These attitudes contribute to your behaviors. For example, if you believe that men should be more dominant or in charge in a relationship, you are more likely to believe that using violence against your partner is justified. Male college students in the United States have reported similar beliefs. Men are more likely than women to think that supporting violence against women is appropriate. Men also may believe that IPV consists of only a small set of behaviors. Female students are more likely to support reporting and criminalizing domestic violence along with supporting responses to IPV from the police. Although limited information is available regarding queer people's attitudes toward IPV, current research findings suggest that IPV is prevalent among LGBTQ individuals.

Other factors exist as well. Your age may also be a predictor of your attitude toward IPV. For example, the younger you are, the more likely you are to be accepting of IPV. Your race and ethnicity may also contribute to individual attitudes or beliefs about IPV. If you are an ethnic minority, you may have more accepting attitudes toward IPV.

Did You Know?

- In the United States, between 8 percent and 12 percent of women are battered by their intimate partners each year. This equates to about one million women.
- In the United States, more than 12 million women and men are victims of IPV each year.
- 25 percent of female college students and 10 percent of male college students report having experienced IPV.

IPV is not isolated to heterosexual relationships. Couples in same-sex relationships can also experience IPV. Sexual minority students are at greater risk of experiencing IPV or sexual assault than their cisgendered, heterosexual counterparts. This is due in part to LGBTQ individuals experiencing confusion and concealing their sexuality, having experienced or anticipating rejection, victimization, discrimination, and internalizing stigmas about their sexuality. In same-sex relationships, 32 percent of LGBTQ individuals have reported physical abuse. Along with physical abuse, 82 percent have reported emotional abuse and 52 percent have reported experiencing threats. Among LGBTQ-identifying college students, rates of IPV remain high—perpetration occurs around 31 percent to 40 percent depending on the type of harm.

When you are in an intimate relationship, you should never feel afraid of your partner. There should also never be an incident where your partner threatens you or hurts you with any form of harm. Finally, you should never feel shamed, worthless, or bad about yourself because of what your partner says or does to you. You deserve to be loved and respected.

What if you are in an abusive relationship? Well, if your partner is doing any of the actions mentioned above, seek help from friends, family, or a professional and leave the relationship. It is important to surround yourself with people you can trust. There may also be a domestic abuse hotline in your area or on your campus. If you feel you are in danger, you can also call 911.

YOUR TURN 5.3

Assessing Intimate Partner Violence

Directions: Review the following questions and statements. This is not meant to be a comprehensive assessment of IPV. Rather, the answers to these questions can help you gauge whether you are in an abusive relationship.

1. Have you ever been emotionally or physically abused by your partner?

2. Within the last year, have you been hit, slapped, kicked, or otherwise physically hurt by your partner?

3. Have you been threatened by your partner?

4. Has your partner forced you to have sex when you did not want to?

5. What happens when you and your partner argue, fight, or have a disagreement?

6. Does your partner use drugs or alcohol? If yes, how do they act when they are drinking or on drugs?

7. Does your partner own a gun or have weapons in their residence? Has your partner ever threatened to use them when they were upset or angry?

Tool Box 5.2

- IPV can occur in any intimate relationship, regardless of sexual orientation.

- Various factors may influence your attitude toward condoning or preventing IPV.

- You should never feel afraid or fearful in a relationship. If you do, reach out to a trusted individual or speak with a counselor to help you figure out options.

5.3: Unwanted Sexual Experience and Sexual Assault

Sexual interactions should bring a sense of pleasure and enable a person to feel fulfilled. However, at times, one may be faced with issues surrounding their sexual health and experiences. Unwanted sexual experience refers to any form of sexual interaction committed against a person without consent. They could be in non-contact (e.g., stalking) or contact (e.g., forceful physical act) forms. Sexual assault is a violent sexual act and/or activity (e.g., rape) toward a person and can take on different forms. It can occur if someone is trying to initiate sexual activity without your consent or despite your refusal. Sexual assault also involves ignoring cues to stop or slow down during sexual activity. Finally, sexual assault is occurring if a person continues to pursue sexual activity or intercourse without checking in with you or while you were still deciding. It should always be your decision to engage in sexual activities, and no one should ever pressure you into doing that. This includes the first time you choose to have sex and every time after that.

YOUR TURN 5.4

Attitudes Toward Sexual Violence

Directions: Take some time to reflect on the following statements and questions regarding your beliefs and attitudes toward sexual violence.

1. What does the term "rape" mean to you?

_____

_____

_____

2. What does the term "sexual harassment" mean to you?

_____

_____

_____

3. Are there any other terms you would associate with sexual abuse?

_____

4. If you became the victim of a sexual assault, would you tell someone? Why or why not?

_____

_____

_____

5. Men cannot be raped.

_____

_____

_____

6. Each woman should be responsible for preventing her own rape.

_____

_____

_____

You may have heard many stories of unwanted sexual experience and sexual assault that happen on college campuses in the form of date-rape drugs. These drugs are put in a drink when a person is distracted. With high doses of the drug, you can lose muscle control and suffer amnesia and a loss of consciousness. The effects of the drugs are heightened with alcohol. You can feel the effects within 30 minutes of ingesting the drug. Here are some methods to protect yourself from date-rape drugs.

1. Never leave your drink somewhere and then come back and drink from it.

2. Do not drink from a punch bowl.

3. Never share a drink or drink something you that you did not open yourself.

4. Be cautious when having a drink with a stranger.

Did You Know?

- Women who attend college are more likely to experience sexual assault than women in the general population.

- Women are more vulnerable to sexual assault in the first or second year of college due to alcohol/drug use, student housing, and parties.

There are some ways that you can protect yourself from sexual assault. Your campus should have security escorts available at your college when it is dark out or when you feel unsafe. Utilize these escorts if you are walking back to your dorm at night. Also, walk in well-lit areas and try to have a friend accompany you if you are out at night. In case you have to go out alone, make sure a friend or roommate knows where you are and check in periodically with each other.

YOUR TURN 5.5 IDENTIFYING SEXUAL ASSAULT

Directions: Take some time to review the questions and statements below. These can help you identify whether you or someone you know has experienced sexual assault.

1. Has someone used physical force or threats of physical force to engage in sexual penetration or oral sex with you? These attempts can either be successful or unsuccessful.

2. Has someone used physical force or threatened physical force to kiss, touch, grab, grope, or rub against you?

3. Has sexual penetration or oral sex happened to you while you were unable to consent or stop what was occurring because you were incapacitated (passed out or asleep)?

4. Has someone kissed, touched, grabbed, groped, or rubbed against you while you were unable to consent or stop what was occurring because you were incapacitated (passed out or asleep)?

5. Has someone kissed or sexually touched you without your active, ongoing voluntary agreement?

If you are sexually assaulted or raped, you should immediately go to the nearest hospital emergency room or student health center. Staff will examine you to collect evidence, so make sure you do not change clothes. Staff will also assist you in contacting the authorities. The perpetrator may do this to someone else, which is why it is important to make a report.

Making a report may be difficult because you may experience feelings of embarrassment, shame, or self-blame. You may also feel that what happened is very personal to you and that it is difficult to relive such a traumatic experience again and again. This is why it is important for you to connect with your college counseling center and speak with a counselor. A counselor can help you talk about your feelings and experience so that you feel supported. Your college counseling center may also have group sessions for survivors of rape and sexual assault.

Tool Box 5.3

- Sexual assault involves any form of sexual contact or behavior that occurs without your consent.
- Date-rape drugs are a form of sexual assault used on college campuses.
- Go to the nearest hospital or student health center if you are sexually assaulted.
- Your college counseling center can provide you with supportive resources if you are sexually assaulted.

VOICES FROM CAMPUS 5.1

A Survivor's Story

As with many stories that I have heard from others, my experience occurred when I was 18 and a freshman in college. Throughout high school, I was sheltered and had many demanding expectations from my parents. So college was a welcomed change. I felt like I was finally able to break free from the social shackles they placed on me.

I started doing what everyone else was doing—drinking. I was drinking a lot. It is embarrassing to admit now, but at the time it felt great to just have no worries and experience what I thought was freedom. Going out on the weekends to parties became routine, and I usually found myself drunk by the time the night was over.

This particular night I was so drunk that I could barely function. I only remember fragments, but I recall being carried upstairs by a guy who decided to stay with me for the night. He said he wanted to stay with me because he was "making sure that I was okay." I forgot to mention that prior to this evening, I was a virgin. Next thing I knew, this guy was on top of me trying to have sex with me. I was so disoriented that it was difficult to fight back, and I remember trying to find the words to tell him to stop.

I'll never forget the feeling when I woke up the next morning—a feeling that so much had just been taken from me. I also felt so ashamed and embarrassed. I never told anyone what happened. Instead, I just held it all in and eventually fell into a deep depression. I tried to kill myself, and my best friend intervened before it was too late. Somehow I told her what happened that night. I remember feeling some relief after finally sharing my story.

My best friend encouraged me to talk with a counselor, so I made an appointment. It was hard at first but my counselor made me feel safe to tell my story. She made me realize that I was strong for just being able to tell my story. I also realized that I was not alone in my experience.

This is an experience that you just never forget. One thing that I have realized over the years is that telling my story helps. It doesn't help me get back what I lost, but I have learned that my story helps others come forward and get the support they need. So if this has happened to you, know that you are a strong and beautiful person. You deserve to be heard and treated with respect.

TAKING CARE OF YOUR MIND AND EMOTIONS

A nxiety and depression are something you hear about a lot. You may have heard that your family members or friends are anxious, unhappy, or sad to the degree that they can't function in everyday life. Some of you you may have experienced these feelings yourself. The thing is anxiety and depression may be closer to you than you think! In this chapter, we discuss how anxiety and depression can affect your life in multiple areas, especially mental health and well-being. We review the symptoms of anxiety and depression and go over risk factors and warning signs for suicide. We also discuss ways in which you can learn to take care of your thoughts and emotions so you can feel better about yourself and develop a more positive outlook on your life.

6.1: Anxiety

Anxiety can be a pest sometimes. It can overwhelm you at the most inconvenient times and seems to come out of nowhere. This is why anxiety can feel like an "attack" to a person who experiences it. Also, like a pest, anxiety can be very difficult to get rid of. Individuals who experience anxiety agree that anxiety is typically with them all the time and they have learned ways to manage it.

Although uncomfortable, experiencing anxiety is a natural biological function. It serves as a warning sign to us when there is anticipated danger or threat. Anxiety is usually associated with something in the future. Anxiety is your body's way of telling you, "Hey, we have a problem here and something is pretty uncertain!" This can be helpful at times, but we as humans can make things even harder for ourselves. In the case of anxiety, we can obsess and attach ourselves to unhelpful thoughts. As a result, the anxiety then becomes excessive and out of the norm for what you are experiencing.

Did You Know?

- 23 percent of college students report anxiety.

YOUR TURN 6.1

What Triggers my Anxiety?

Directions: Take a few moments to make a list of some of the people, places, or things that trigger your anxiety. How do you respond to each of your triggers?

Trigger 1: _____

How I respond:

_____

_____

Trigger 2: _____

How I respond:

_____

_____

Trigger 3: _____
How I respond:

_____

_____

There are different triggers when it comes to anxiety. However, one of the most common forms of anxiety that you may experience in college is known as social anxiety disorder. The common feature in social anxiety disorder is an intense fear or anxiety during a social situation or interaction where you may be scrutinized by others. Think about all the moments in which this may happen during your college experience. For example, you may have to give a presentation in front of a class or you may feel a lot of pressure to perform well as a musician or athlete. Another example is that you feel like all eyes are on you when walking into a party.

Along with social anxiety, you may experience periods of generalized anxiety. This occurs when you experience excessive anxiety and worry about many different events or activities. Too often, this anxiety or worry is completely out of proportion to the likelihood of what you think may happen or how bad the outcome will be. As a young adult in college, you may worry about managing all your responsibilities such as getting assignments done, meeting deadlines, studying for exams, working, and paying bills and tuition. Some of these worries are manageable. Generalized anxiety disorder starts to develop when these worries become more distressing, last longer, and occur more frequently without anything seeming to trigger the anxiety.

There are several factors that put you at risk for experiencing anxiety, particularly on campus. You may feel yourself having to be more competitive amongst your peers for the best grades. This can be especially true if you are already looking ahead to further your education in graduate school. Having a perfectionistic attitude has been shown to put you at risk for developing anxiety. This is a result of avoiding personal failure, setting unrealistic standards for yourself, and being driven by a fear of failure rather than achieving success. You may also face fierce competition to attain top spots in other activities such as sports or theater/dance. Anxiety can be common if you identify with an underrepresented or marginalized population. This level of anxiety increases if you have also experienced discrimination and lack a peer support system.

Tool Box 6.1

- Anxiety is a natural biological function.
- The way we think and perceive situations can create excessive anxiety.
- A variety of social pressures and personality traits can create unrealistic expectations and lead to excessive anxiety.

6.2: Depression

Depression refers to an intense feeling of sadness, hopelessness, or lack of interest. Depression can feel completely debilitating at times. You can feel like each moment is a major hurdle to get through. At times, you feel as though it is impossible to get your mind and body moving because you feel stuck—stuck in a blanket that shields you from the world but is causing pain at the same time. It is also a known fact that depression is commonly accompanied by anxiety. In other words, individuals with depression typically experience symptoms of depression (e.g., feeling of sadness, loss of interest) simultaneously with other symptoms of anxiety (e.g., faster heartbeat, excessive worries).

Depression can be mistaken for sadness and grief. However, depression is not an emotion in and of itself. In fact, depression is the loss of feelings—you are unable to experience a wide variety of emotions including excitement, joy, disappointment, and sadness. Depression is an illness that affects you as a whole person. Depression affects your body, thoughts, feelings, and behaviors. Depression can change the way you think, making you feel worthless and weak. It can harm your relationships and deprive you of any sense of confidence. Due to its crippling effects, depression can feel as though nothing will help you get better or that it is pointless to seek help.

Did You Know?

- One out of four college students suffer from a form of mental illness, including depression.

- 44 percent of U.S. college students report having symptoms of depression.
- More than 80 percent of U.S. college students felt overwhelmed by all they had to do in the past year.
- U.S. college students identified depression and anxiety as among the top barriers to performing well in college.

The telltale sign of depression is that you feel a persistently sad or empty mood. This can also be experienced as tension or anxiety. In fact, there is a high degree of overlap between depressive and anxious symptoms. If you are experiencing depression, you may go about your daily routine of work, school, and play but these activities seem incredibly hollow. If you are going through a major depressive episode, you are probably withdrawing from these activities altogether because you feel unproductive and cannot focus. Other notable symptoms include significant weight loss, difficulty thinking or concentrating nearly every day, having little to no interest in pleasurable activities, and feelings of worthlessness or thoughts of death or suicide.

Fortunately, around 80–90 percent of people experiencing depression can be treated, with significantly positive results. The thing is, not all of them seek professional help. Would it surprise you to know that only one person in three who suffer from depression seeks treatment? This is mainly because of the stigma attached to depression, which includes viewing individuals who are depressed as having some sort of character flaw.

Now that we have reviewed both anxiety and depression, let's talk about what you can do when you feel anxious or depressed. The reality is you will never be able to fully protect yourself from experiencing anxiety or depression. It is important to know the warning signs and symptoms and develop healthy coping skills to reduce the frequency, duration, or intensity of your anxiety or depression.

If you are experiencing symptoms of depression or anxiety that are interfering with your ability to focus on your studies and have a healthy social life, seek help. Treatment works if you are motivated and commit to the process. It is okay to ask for help, so do not beat yourself up if you cannot manage it on your own. As a college student, it can seem impossible to find the time to make and keep appointments, but you need to make the effort to seek help.

Check out your college website for information regarding mental health services. These services may be found through on-campus counseling centers or a student health center. It may also be a good idea to make an appointment with a doctor. Your physician can help rule out other health problems that may be contributing to your depression or anxiety. If your doctor rules out additional health problems, she can make a referral to a mental health professional such as a psychiatrist or counselor for treatment.

Now that you have a referral, how is depression or anxiety treated? Both conditions can be treated with a combination of medications and talk therapy. There are a wide variety of medications that have been found to be effective in treating both anxiety and depression. Talk therapy includes personalized situations in which the counselor can help you understand, identify, and manage your thoughts and feelings. The counselor will help you identify and replace the negative thoughts that are contributing to your symptoms. You will also be guided in building confidence in yourself so you can find solutions to your own problems. Remember that it is important to seek out help sooner rather than later since both anxiety and depression can be seen as "progressive" diseases, which means the symptoms only get worse over time. As a result, it can create a profound impact on your life and at times continue to interfere with many aspects of daily life. Alternative forms of therapy such as art or play therapy can also help a person express her feelings when she may not be able to articulate such feelings through words.

There are also additional strategies you can incorporate into your daily routine to manage anxiety and depression. Regular exercise has significant benefits to your overall mental and physical health—even if you just get out and walk for around 20–30 minutes per day. Try to keep a consistent sleep schedule and make sure you are getting enough sleep—so avoid those all-night study sessions before taking exams. It is also important to spend time with friends and do fun things that help you feel fulfilled in life. Campuses have a wide variety of resources, so make sure you are informed about these resources. You may be able to find student support groups where you can connect with and feel supported by other students struggling with the same issues. You should not feel that seeking treatment or professional help is a sign of weakness. Rather, by helping yourself, you are putting yourself on a path toward success in college.

Tool Box 6.2

- Depression affects almost half of college students.
- If left untreated, depression can affect every aspect of your life.
- Depression and anxiety can be treated with counseling, medication, or a combination of both treatments.
- It is okay to ask for help, and those who seek help often report significant improvements.

6.3: Suicide

Suicide can be a difficult topic to talk about. Some of you may have had family or friends who have attempted or completed suicide. You may have also tried to harm yourself in the past. Either way, this is a topic that should be discussed so you can identify the warning signs and know what steps to take if you or someone you know is threatening to harm themselves.

As with any other concept presented in this chapter, it is important to understand what suicide is and how it is defined. Suicide refers to a death that occurs from self-inflicted behaviors (e.g., shooting, cutting) accompanied with intent to die. A suicide attempt is a self-injurious behavior in which there was intent to die but a nonfatal outcome occurred. Another term you may hear concerning the topic of suicide is suicide ideation, which refers to having thoughts about engaging in suicidal behavior.

Did You Know?

- There are more than 1,000 suicides on college campuses every year.
- About 0.5–7.5 percent of college students complete suicide.
- Suicide was the leading cause of death for college students in 2011.
- Between 15 and 18 percent of college students report suicidal thoughts.

YOUR TURN 6.2

Misconceptions about Suicide

Directions: As with many types of mental health topics, suicide comes with its own set of myths and misunderstandings. Take some time to review common statements about suicide and reflect on whether you believe them to be true or not. Answers are provided at the end of the exercise.

1. Suicide occurs without warning.
2. Suicide affects all social classes.
3. All suicidal people are deeply depressed.
4. Women are more likely to attempt suicide than men.
5. Suicide is an inherited condition passed down from generation to generation.

Answers: 1. False, 2. True, 3. False, 4. True, 5. False

Studies have found that it is more common among undergraduates than graduate students to report suicidal thoughts. This may be due to the transition from high school to college typically being more difficult than the transition from undergraduate to graduate studies. College students have to adjust to various demands including academic, career, interpersonal, and personal life with little life experience, and sometimes they are less informed about choices and solutions. For example, you may be an international or first-generation student who is trying to adapt to a mainstream culture in a U.S. college campus. In addition, you may be an ethnic or a sexual minority or a nontraditional student who is either working full time or commuting. You may experience some forms of disabilities. These issues can leave you feeling isolated and removed from others.

There are factors that put you at increased risk for suicide. If you are feeling hopeless or depressed, you should reach out to people you can trust. Individuals who have poor coping skills and problem-solving techniques are also at higher risk for suicide. If you are currently struggling with drug or alcohol use, this puts you at increased risk for suicide as well. If you or someone you know is making comments indicating that they do not feel they have a reason to live or are feeling pessimistic or hopeless about the future, help should be sought immediately. Below is a list of potential risk factors for suicide.

Depression
Other mental disorders
Physical pain
Feelings of rejection
Feelings of failure
Feelings of hopelessness
Feelings of self-blame
Family history of suicide
Family violence
Family sexual abuse
Migration from another country
Substance use disorder
Breakup with recent partner
Academic pressure
Social isolation
Financial problems
Legal difficulties

You may feel hesitant about getting help from campus mental health services. In addition to experiencing the stigma of suicide, there are other reasons that college students do not seek mental health services on campus. Those reasons include one's attitudes or beliefs about mental illness or mental health services, personal difficulty disclosing sensitive information, and fear that the information shared will be included in your academic records. Fortunately, campus mental health services have been trying to educate students and families to reduce the stigma of suicide and mental illness, as well as increase knowledge of suicide and allow people to share personal experiences.

Did You Know?

- Students at high risk of suicide often do not seek help.

- 80 percent of college students who died of suicide did not reach out for help.

Life satisfaction has been shown to be a protective factor against suicide. This includes standards that you hold toward yourself. Some examples include having a job, close friends, or achieving academic goals. Life satisfaction is a protective factor because your standards can create a sense of purpose in life. This sense of purpose in life can assist in creating a buffer if you are feeling depressed. As we discussed earlier, when you feel depressed, you create negative thought patterns and behaviors that cause you to act in self-destructive ways. Having a sense of meaning and purpose in life can help build a defense against these thoughts and behaviors.

Tool Box 6.3

- There are many myths and stigmas related to suicide which often prevent people from seeking help.

- It is important to educate yourself and be aware of the warning signs and risk factors that contribute to suicide.

- Having increased life satisfaction, meaning, and purpose in life are significant protective factors against suicide.

YOUR TURN 6.3

Self-Esteem

Take a moment to reflect on and answer the following statements:

1. When I reflect on the last four years, here is what I am proud of:

_____

_____

_____

2. List some of the ways that you show respect for yourself.

_____

_____

_____

3. When I think of the positive qualities that I have, these are some that come to mind:

_____

_____

_____

4. These are the times when I feel useless:

_____

_____

_____

After answering all of the questions above, what do you notice with your answers? Were there questions that were easier or harder to answer than others? If so, why?

All of these questions describe some aspect of your self-esteem. But what exactly is self-esteem? Self-esteem is recognized as either having an overall positive or negative view of yourself. Your self-esteem is made up of all the perceptions you have about yourself and the judgments you make. For example, do you think you are physically attractive? How confident do you feel? Do you feel people enjoy being around you because of your personality? Self-esteem is important because it can lead to favorable or unfavorable outcomes in your life and, more specifically, during your college experience. For example, having higher self-esteem is linked to having more motivation to learn and higher academic outcomes. On the other side of the coin, low self-esteem has been shown to lead to dropping out of school, poor grades, financial problems, or isolating from friends and peers.

Having a stronger sense of self and higher self-esteem can act as a buffer when you encounter stressful events that will inevitably pop up for you. But why would self-esteem be important? Think about it this way—if you look at yourself as being worthless or incompetent, you are less likely to work through the issue because you do not have the confidence that you can overcome the situation. Instead, you avoid the situation by procrastinating or even turning to drugs or alcohol as a means of escape. This only makes the problem worse and, as a result, you feel more worthless—and then the cycle just continues. This is why college students who have low self-esteem often report suffering from depression.

You are also more likely to feel as though you can handle a stressful event when you have increased self-esteem. You will not feel threatened by a situation; instead of avoiding, you will adapt to the situation using positive coping skills. Often, we try to avoid stressful situations hoping they will go away—many times they will not. So you have to ask yourself, "How do I *work with* this situation?"

One of the ways you can increase your self-esteem is to be more optimistic—easier said than done. Having a positive outlook on life and about yourself can be especially useful when encountering adverse situations. Findings from studies have shown that people who have a more optimistic attitude also report having higher self-esteem. This is because self-esteem is affected by your expectations for the future. If you have a more positive mindset, you will not feel the effects of a stressful event so strongly. In other words, you become more resilient. This means you can recover from conditions more quickly or withstand them altogether.

Tool Box 6.4

- Self-esteem includes the values and perceptions you have about yourself.
- Self-esteem has been shown to be a protective factor against stressful events during college.
- Having a more optimistic outlook can increase your overall self-esteem.

6.4: Unplugging From Technology

Technology has certainly made our lives easier. At the click of a button you can purchase an item or send a message to someone on the other side of the world. Think of what you can do with a few apps on your smartphone. You can order a meal ahead of time, pay for it, and use a built-in GPS to drive to the restaurant and pick up your meal—all with a few clicks and swipes with your finger.

Think about how much time and energy you spend connected to your phone, laptop, tablet, or computer. Around 88 percent of teens in the United States have access to a mobile phone, and 73 percent of those teens have a smartphone. In addition to phones, 87 percent of teens have access to a desktop or laptop. Can you guess what percentage of you report going online daily? Try 92 percent—yes, you read that correctly. Ninety-two percent of teens report going online daily. And if you are one of those teens, you are probably visiting multiple social media sites in addition to sending an average of 30–40 text messages a day.

Unfortunately, all this convenience has come at a price—our reliance on this technology. We feel we need to always be plugged in just to make us feel like we are being "productive" and connected with each other. Being tethered to our gadgets makes us feeling constantly "on," which can leave us feeling mentally and emotionally exhausted. We spend our free time browsing social media, always comparing ourselves to the lives of others, making us feel anxious or depressed. You may spend lots of time on the computer working on projects or writing papers only to find yourself lounging on the couch in front of the TV as "downtime." How ironic that we supplement one form of technology for another. It's time to change this routine!

We realize that it can almost be impossible to unplug from technology altogether. That is not our focus in this section. Rather, we encourage you to take time—even just moments in the day—to turn off your gadgets and spend time with yourself or in activities that help you express yourself and are fulfilling. There are probably many activities you could find to help you unplug from your gadgets, and research shows that there are significant health benefits from putting those gadgets away. Twenty minutes of walking or silent meditation can have significant benefits to your overall health. Adult coloring books have been growing in popularity and can be an excellent way to help your mind refresh from a stressful day. Try picking up a good book to read and let your mind get lost in another world. Consider making plans with friends for the evening or weekend where you have a game night or spend time at a nearby park.

Tool Box 6.5

- Young adults spend a significant amount of time using technology and social media.
- Using computers, smartphones, or social media for extended periods of time can lead to increased physical and emotional problems.
- Taking brief or extended periods of time to get away from electronic gadgets can have beneficial outcomes on your overall health.

VOICES FROM CAMPUS 6.1

A New Start

How does the saying go? "Be careful what you wish for." When I was searching for colleges, I knew that I wanted to go to a large state college. The larger the campus, the more opportunities to meet new people. This would be a welcomed change from my small-town high school—or so I thought. I knew myself pretty well and although I was more of an introvert, I thought a larger campus would help get me out of my shell.

The first semester in college was overwhelming to say the least. I felt completely swallowed up by the experience. Yes, there were more people than I could have imagined, but I found myself having a hard time meeting and talking with new people. So instead of taking risks and talking with people, I withdrew. I just stayed in my room all the time and found myself sinking into an endless abyss of sadness. I noticed that I was not feeling anything anymore. There was just this emotional void. Eventually, I just stopped caring altogether and could not find the energy or motivation to get up for class. This caused my grades to plunge, and I felt myself falling farther down the depression abyss.

My parents came to visit and we talked about options. I was getting close to finishing up the year so they recommended that I move back home and attend a community college. They insisted that I go to treatment because they were worried that moving to a smaller college was not the entire solution. I reluctantly agreed.

It took some time to adjust to the campus, but I noticed myself feeling more comfortable in a smaller environment. I also enjoyed talking with my counselor. She and I were able to find other issues that were causing me to feel depressed. I realized that my self-esteem and confidence were really low, and through counseling I was able to find more confidence in myself. The smaller campus also helped make it easier to make friends and I found myself not just being able to feel again, but feel happier.

Now I am entering my junior year of college, working, and have an internship lined up. I still visit my counselor on a regular basis even if I am not experiencing depression. I look at counseling as a way to take care of myself even if things aren't "wrong" with me.

My advice to all of you who are about to enter college is to think about where you want to go and what environment will really help you reach your potential. Don't be afraid to ask for help because it could just save your life and give you a fresh start.

TAKING CARE OF YOUR RELATIONSHIPS

"Relationship" … what does this really mean? When you put "relationship" in the context of human relations, relationship refers to the way in which people are connected. There is no doubt that a relationship is one of the most important aspects of one's life, from birth to death. In early life, infants need to have a relationship with their caretakers to fulfill their basic and survival needs. As life progresses, friendships help children thrive and grow. Children love being surrounded by and learning from other children and adults who care about them. Teenagers want to be a part of their peer groups and feel like they belong. Young adults seek to have intimate relationships to fulfill their needs for love and a life companion. Later in life, having healthy relationships can help your mind stay active and stimulated. Toward the end of life, having someone with you in one of the last moments is a precious gift.

The thing is, being connected to someone is more complicated than you think. There are infinite levels and layers in each relationship, as well as complex factors impacting such connections. In this chapter, we discuss how social relationships play a vital role in your overall health. We review the importance of staying connected with others and avoiding isolation. We also discuss how the quality of your relationships with others impacts your overall mental health and explore what constitutes a healthy or unhealthy relationship. Finally, we discuss ways in which you can increase your social connections on campus.

7.1: Isolation

Human beings are social creatures. We thrive when we are surrounded by and have meaningful relationships with others. Although we still do not fully understand our social nature, we know that human beings have a biological need for social connectedness. In the movie *Cast Away*, Tom Hanks plays Chuck Noland, a man deserted on an uncharted island after his plane crashes. Chuck spends years on this island alone, learning how to survive. During this time, Chuck finds a volleyball from the aircraft wreckage and paints a face on it, eventually naming it Wilson. Chuck converses with Wilson as if the volleyball were actually talking to him. Due to his isolation, Chuck had an innate drive to make an inanimate object possess human-like qualities so he did not feel alone. That speaks of the innate human need to be connected to others.

Although periods of alone time and spending time with ourselves can be healthy and relieve stress, prolonged isolation can lead to many adverse health consequences. One of the reasons that isolation is unhealthy for human beings is because it can result in chronic stress. The longer we isolate ourselves, the longer the stress affects our bodies physically and mentally. For example, physical stress may impact your immune system making it harder for your body to fight off illnesses and recover. Having close social ties can help reduce the risk of high blood pressure (a precursor to other serious health complications) and weight gain or obesity. People who have a lack of social connectedness often report depression and increased mortality. Then you begin to feel depressed when you do not feel well physically.

Developing friendships can serve many purposes—you will have someone to talk with when facing challenges (or when you just want to chat), company when going on vacation, and support when you need it. When individuals find themselves feeling alone, it can be harmful to their psychological health. Feelings of isolation or a lack of belongingness are directly related to suicidal ideation. Suicide is the second leading cause of death among college students. The highest risk factor associated with suicide is difficulties with interpersonal relationships. Students who experience social isolation and lack of social support and social connectedness are at increased risk of developing suicidal ideation given the emotional and psychological pain that is associated with those experiences.

On the other hand, meaningful connections with others can improve your health and lead to longevity. If you think about avoiding those family holiday gatherings, think again! Even though you may at times find yourself being overwhelmed by those events, being surrounded by family and friends who genuinely love you is important. Fulfilling relationships can serve as your social support during stressful moments. Caring for others also releases stress-reducing hormones.

As you progress through your college experience, you are likely to develop connections in three categories: your family, peers, and academic institution. Emotional support from your family can act as a buffer against the stress, depression, and uncertainty that comes with transitioning to college life. Your family can be a great resource to help you navigate problems that come up in your relationships. If you feel disconnected from your peers, you are likely to start isolating yourself which could lead to suicidal thoughts. Additionally, a lack of engagement on campus can result in depressive symptoms.

Unfortunately, many of us have felt the cold sting of rejection at some point in our lives—whether on the school playground in second grade or on prom night in high school. It happens to us all. Studies have shown that when we experience rejection, our cortisol (stress hormone) levels increase. This feeling of rejection can trigger chronic stress. Fortunately, the same studies have shown that for people with more friends or closer relationships, levels of cortisol were lower after experiencing rejection. This is another example of how friendships can be beneficial to our overall physical and mental health.

Some of you may still be close friends with someone you met in grade school while others may just be developing friendships. Naturally, some friends come and go and some relationships fade away due to life circumstances. However, some friendships may last your entire life. Technology and the Internet have made it more convenient than ever to stay close with those we care about regardless of where they live. So be sure not to let distance keep you from nurturing those friendships. Just because your friend lives on the other side of the country does not necessarily mean you feel the emotional distance.

Although the Internet and social media have made it easier to meet and connect with people, they have some downsides. For example, if you are not entirely comfortable with your social skills, it may seem easier to use the Internet to talk with people and avoid feeling lonely. However, socializing with others face to face may be a challenge for you. If you struggle with social anxiety, you might resort to social media apps like Facebook or Twitter to avoid feeling anxious. This could be helpful at first, but you may develop a tendency to rely on social media too heavily. As a result, you do not take as many risks to get out there and present yourself or deal with real-life situations. While it may feel like you are getting relief from anxiety on social media, you are really just putting a band-aid on a broken leg. You are not dealing with the real source of the problem causing your loneliness. It is important that you engage with others in a personal context so you can work through any feelings of anxiety or insecurity that you have about yourself.

Did You Know?

- In a study with more than 309,000 people, those who reported few strong relationships had an increased risk of premature death by 50 percent, which is the same as smoking up to 15 cigarettes per day.
- Young adults who reported high social media use also reported greater feelings of social isolation.

YOUR TURN 7.1

Am I Lonely?

Directions: Below is a list of statements that are associated with loneliness. Read each statement and select how often those statements occur.

1.	I isolate myself from others	Often	Sometimes	Rarely	Never
2.	I have a hard time being alone	Often	Sometimes	Rarely	Never
3.	I feel excluded from others	Often	Sometimes	Rarely	Never
4.	People do not know me very well	Often	Sometimes	Rarely	Never
5.	I have trouble making friends	Often	Sometimes	Rarely	Never
6.	I wait around for people to call or text me back	Often	Sometimes	Rarely	Never
7.	When I do things alone, I feel unhappy	Often	Sometimes	Rarely	Never
8.	I am around people but they do not share the same interests	Often	Sometimes	Rarely	Never

Tool Box 7.1

- Human beings are social creatures with a desire for belonging and companionship.
- Taking time out to be alone can be healthy, but prolonged isolation can lead to many negative health consequences.
- Rejection is a natural experience when trying to meet new people or make new friends.
- Social media and the Internet can be helpful in dealing with social anxiety. Prolonged use can lead to deficits in social skills and increased isolation.

7.2: Quality vs. Quantity

Before delving into whether it is important to have many friends or just a few friends, it is helpful to understand what friendship really is. The overall consensus reveals that friendship is composed of numerous aspects. First, it is a voluntary relationship between two people. In a friendship, no one should ever feel forced to engage or interact with another person. Second, friendships are personal—you may share some level of emotional intimacy and provide support to the other person. Finally, friendships result in the development of trust so that you both feel safe to disclose information.

You may be questioning why you should have friends and strive for healthy relationships. One of the biggest reasons is that life can throw some really tough situations at us, if you have not already noticed. Friendships can be a solid basis for your ability to cope with those challenging situations as you progress through college—and rest assured, they will happen. Often, you may feel like you just want to have some time alone when you are going through a terrible experience. However, knowing that you have a friend who cares about you and is willing to help you get through such an experience is comforting.

So how many friends should you have? In the age of social media, you could feel like you need a large number of friends to feel important or supported. You may think that you should be accepting lots of friend requests on Facebook or that your Twitter account should have lots of followers. Social media puts a lot of pressure on us to expand our social networks.

There is nothing wrong with having many friends and acquaintances. However, you want to make sure that you have close relationships that you can rely on—people who will be there for you through the toughest of times. This can only be achieved if you nurture close relationships. Give yourself a break if you feel guilty when you tend to be selective with who you choose to let in and trust. This will serve you better in the long run when you need help and support.

Did You Know?

- People with quality friendships are more likely to be better adjusted, feel more competent, and have higher self-esteem.

- Quality friendships lead to greater life satisfaction, ability to cope with stressors, and satisfaction of needs.

- People with quality relationships are less likely to experience depression, suicidal ideation, loneliness, and social isolation.

YOUR TURN 7.2

My Important Relationships

Directions: Take some time to reflect on the relationships that are most meaningful to you right now. Think about what you bring to the relationship that enhances your connection to that person. Then write down things that the other person brings to the relationship.

Name of person	This is what I bring to the relationship	This is what they bring to the relationship

Tool Box 7.2

- It is more important to focus on quality of relationships versus quantity of relationships.
- Social media and culture can make you feel as though you need to have many friends.
- Quality relationships will be key in helping you work through challenging situations during college.

7.3: Healthy vs. Unhealthy

How do you know that you have a healthy relationship with a friend, partner, or family member? One of the ways you can tell is if you sense that the other person has a desire for what is best for you. They want to see that you are in a good place in your life and are willing to help you get there. Sometimes they may even need to give you some "tough love" by telling you things you may need to hear. For example, your friend may see that your drinking is becoming a problem and they may confront you because they are concerned. This is where honesty and trust come into play. Being honest with one another may cause some initial tension, but that is much easier to resolve than feelings of doubt and betrayal that stem from lies and dishonesty.

Healthy relationships comprise two other essential ingredients: sympathy and empathy. You may think of them as the same but they are entirely different. Sympathy usually involves feelings of sorrow for someone who is experiencing some type of misfortune. For example, you may send a card if you hear that someone has experienced a death in the family. Empathy focuses on one's ability to imagine themselves in the situation of another, experiencing the emotions or thoughts of the other person. Using the example above, a sympathetic statement might be, "I'm sorry for your loss" while an empathetic statement might sound like, "I can't imagine how hard this loss has been for you." Both ingredients are equally important in a relationship because some moments you feel comforted when someone reaches out during a time of suffering while other moments you may need someone who can understand what you are going through.

On a similar note, relationships that are healthy and fulfilling involve a shared understanding built around compassion. Compassion refers to the love and concern that you have for another person. This can only be generated when you go to one another for emotional support. During these moments, you may feel vulnerable about sharing your thoughts and feelings. This is why it is important that you feel safe in the relationship to be yourself and to express your thoughts and feelings without being worried you will be judged or criticized.

Healthy relationships should lead you to feel energized. If you are in a relationship where you constantly feel emotionally drained or frustrated with the other person, chances are it may not be a healthy dynamic. Along with feeling energized, you should feel a sense of empowerment from your friendships. True friends will encourage you and make you feel like you can overcome obstacles. Also you feel better about yourself through these relationships. Friendships should remind you of the best qualities about yourself.

Healthy relationships are reciprocal in nature. This means that the relationship is built on a shared understanding of "give and take." Both parties should be putting in an effort, and hopefully the same amount of effort, in the relationship. Some moments you may need more attention in the relationship, and at other times the other party is in need of more support. It is also important not to keep score in the relationship. Keeping tabs on when and how much support you give will only breed resentment and contempt, which are completely toxic to a relationship.

Finally, a true friendship will make you feel like you want more connection with that particular person. As this connection builds, you learn more about your sense of self and the other person. Relationships are fundamental to how we form our identities—our beliefs about ourselves. Make sure you stay connected to people who love, value, and appreciate you for who you are and what you bring to the relationship.

Did You Know?

- Healthy relationships are a great source of social support, which leads to increased self-esteem and reduces depression.
- Social support can lessen worries or concerns by turning negative emotions into positive ones—this can be helpful in coping with stressful experiences.

YOUR TURN 7.3

Is My Relationship Healthy?

Directions: It is important that you take time out to reflect on your current relationships. Use the following activity to evaluate whether you have friendships that are healthy or unhealthy for you. Think of a specific friend that you have in your life right now. Then, read each item below and select those items which capture the relationship.

Friend's name:_____

___My friend helps me solve problems

___I can't really rely on my friend to help me solve problems

___My friend never breaks a promise

___My friend can never keep a promise

___My friend never lies to me

___I can never believe what my friend says

___My friend makes me feel safe

___I feel anxious or uneasy when I'm with my friend

___My friend and I share our experiences

___I usually never know what is going on with my friend

___ My friend can forgive me

___My friend can never let things go when I make a mistake

___My friend treats me with respect

___I feel low about myself when I am with my friend

___I can be honest with my friend

___I feel uncomfortable speaking my mind with my friend

If you selected more items on the left-hand side, then you have the qualities of a healthy relationship. If you selected more items on the right-hand side, then you may not have a healthy relationship. Spend some time and reflect on why that may be the case.

YOUR TURN 7.4

Assessing My Friendship

Directions: Let's take some more time and reflect on specific friendships in your life right now. Again, select a specific friend of yours. Read each statement and respond.

1. If I were in a new situation, _____ would make me feel

_____

_____

2. If _____ and I did not see each other for a few months, we would

_____

_____

3. I just had a fight with _____. Afterwards, we will

_____

_____

4. There is something very personal that I have not told

_____ yet. If I told _____, they

would probably respond by _____

_____

_____

5. I just had an awful experience. If I reach out to _____

I know they will respond by _____

_____

_____

6. I am in a situation where I feel very uncomfortable, nervous, or

scared. _____ would make me feel _____

_____

_____ by doing _____

_____

_____

Tool Box 7.3

- Both healthy and unhealthy relationships can lead to significant mental health consequences.

- Unhealthy relationships can lead to increased stress, depression, substance use, and lower self-esteem.

- Healthy relationships are composed of many qualities, including sympathy, empathy, desire for growth in one another, feeling energized, mutual respect and compassion, and physical and emotional safety.

7.4: Engagement

If you are new on campus, you may not know anyone. Chances are you may be feeling really overwhelmed and intimidated. How on earth are you going to meet new people? Well, fortunately for you, college provides an enormous amount of opportunity to meet people because you are surrounded by hundreds, if not thousands, of your peers who are just as interested in meeting people as you are. You just have to know where to look and what resources are available. More importantly, it is up to you to take the initiative.

Let's start with one of the obvious ways to meet people—in class! There's no way around it—if you want to graduate, you will have to attend class. While some classes may be a pain, they are also an excellent opportunity to meet new people. Classes that are part of your major will also be a way to meet people with similar interests. Don't hesitate to strike up a conversation with the student next to you. Some classes may require group projects, which is another way to connect and develop friendships. This is true even if you are enrolled in an online degree program. You can meet your classmates virtually and start to form meaningful relationships with them.

You will have the option of joining a fraternity/sorority, club, or student organization. These places offer many opportunities for you not only to meet new people but also to explore different extracurricular activities. So take some time to research the different organizations and see which ones attract your interest. Either way, these organizations provide endless opportunities to socialize and meet others.

If you decide to work while you are attending classes, consider finding a job on campus. There are always lots of part-time job opportunities, whether it is working at a campus recreation center or in the library. These are ways to earn extra income and meet people, not just your peers but faculty and staff. Networking with faculty and staff on campus can be a great way to secure an internship in the future.

At some point in time, there is usually an event or activity that is happening on your campus. Campus events provide opportunities to meet new people of all different ethnicities and cultures. These events may target a personal or professional interest of yours. So be sure to check out bulletin boards around campus. Your college may also have a newspaper that lists upcoming events. Since you will be new to campus, you might be required to participate in orientation. Usually, orientation lasts about a week. This is a helpful way to not only get you acquainted with your campus but also with other students as well.

Social media can be a great tool to locate and promote activities. Your campus may have a Facebook or Twitter page that can direct you to new events. There may even be specific Facebook pages for your class and major. For example, "University of (fill in the blank) Psychology class of 2025." Meetup.org is a great website that lists various groups that meet regularly. There are a wide variety of groups to choose from. You can even start your own group based on a personal or professional interest.

Depending on your school and work schedule, you may have time to volunteer with a cause or organization. Volunteering is an ideal way to connect with like-minded people. Campuses are full of clubs and student organizations that are always looking for new members to help with projects such as building a house for the homeless or organizing a food drive for the food bank. If your faith or spirituality is an important piece in your life, there may be faith-based or community groups on campus that you can connect with.

If you are living in a residence hall on campus, try to get to know people in your building or on your floor. This may happen naturally as you come and go throughout your day. Take some time to stop by people's rooms and introduce yourself. You can even spend some time in the common room and talk to others. Also, it is always helpful to get to know your "neighbor" in case of emergency or when you need immediate assistance from someone.

YOUR TURN 7.5

How Can I Meet People?

Directions: Review the table below of the different ways that you can meet new people and make friends. Take some time to identify the pros and cons for each scenario. This will help you get a better sense of what activities you may feel comfortable with in order to meet others.

Activity	Pros	Cons
Living in a residence hall		
Volunteering		
Social media (Facebook, Twitter, Meetup.org, etc.)		
Religious/spiritual campus event		
Political campus event		
Talking with classmates/ group activity		
Campus job		
Fraternity/sorority		
Parties		

Activity	Pros	Cons
Research opportunity with faculty		
Internships		

Did You Know?

- Developing friendships with individuals of different backgrounds can lead to decreased anxiety and lower expectations of rejection.
- Having friends from other cultures and backgrounds can increase your sense of multiculturalism and your commitment to the environment and social justice. It will also give you a greater understanding of race.

Tool Box 7.4

- It is natural to feel overwhelmed and anxious about making friends in college.
- Campuses provide many opportunities to meet new people.
- It is up to you to take the initiative to put yourself out there and try to build new friendships.

No Place Like Home

Although we may wish, there are just no quick fixes. I remember my first year away at college all too well. I decided to move away from home and attend a large campus mainly because I just needed to get away from the turmoil and stress at home. I had always had rocky relationships with my parents. They were good people but sometimes we just didn't see eye to eye. High school was an enjoyable but draining experience. I made really wonderful friends, but the drama just became too much for me. I thought that moving 500 miles away would solve my problems and I could just meet new people and have a fresh start.

I consider myself to be a social butterfly. It is not difficult for me to walk into a situation and just casually strike up a conversation with someone. I figured with all the opportunities on campus to meet people, there should be no problems talking with people and making friends. But something happened the moment I stepped out of my car and pulled out the first box to unpack. It hit me that for the very first time in my life, I was really alone. Suddenly, the excitement about a fresh start and new opportunities turned into complete anxiety.

This anxiety would evolve into depression. I started to only leave my room when I had to attend class. I could barely get out a word if someone next to me tried to just strike up a conversation in class. People would stop by my dorm to say hi and invite me to events or parties. I can remember putting on a fake smile and nodding that I would attend only to have to come up with a lie the next day about why I did not show up.

I tried reaching out to my high school friends through Facebook. I wondered if they were having similar experiences. But reading all their posts and messages only forced me more into retreat, mainly because I felt like we were already drifting apart. It seemed like they were turning into different people. But were they? Was I the one changing? Or did I really ever know them at all?

I started to realize that maybe something deeper was going on inside of me beyond not wanting to meet people. Perhaps I did not really know myself as well as I thought I did. Perhaps leaving home to escape the turmoil in my family was merely that—just an escape. And as much as I did not want to admit it to myself, I missed my family. In that moment, I picked up the phone to call home.

I can remember the sense of relief after I hung up the phone with my parents. They told me about their own experiences of being on their own for the first time. My dad talked about how he managed after leaving home at 18, and my mom shared her experience of going away for college after living in a small town all her life. In that moment, I felt like there was possibility. To what end? I had absolutely no clue. But it was better than feeling paralyzed and like I had no options. When someone came by my room with an invitation, I followed through and went. When someone struck up a conversation with me in class, I pushed myself to say more and ask questions.

It took some time but I gradually found my way. Through trial and error, I learned who I felt more comfortable to be around and who I felt safe to talk to. Meeting others helped expose me to so many different interests that I never realized I had. Eventually, I was the one knocking on dorm room doors inviting people to events. I was the one striking up conversations with someone next to me. I started finding myself again.

I know some of you out there can relate to my story and others won't. Some of the ways that I overcame loneliness may help you or they may not. Here is what I learned though. Dealing with loneliness can be one of the most important life skills. Why? Because it forces you to figure out who you want to be and, more importantly, who you want to be with. Loneliness pushes you to examine and learn more about yourself. You have to answer the tough questions—Who am I? What do I want? What do I need from others? How do I fit in?

Don't expect this to be fixed overnight. There are no shortcuts or quick fixes to dealing with loneliness. Counseling and self-help books can be a great tool to get you started but when it comes to figuring out yourself, it is all uncharted territory. Keep pushing yourself and take it one day at a time. You'll be glad you did.

CHAPTER 8

TAKING CARE OF YOUR SPIRIT

As we come to the end of this book, we are going to take a look at one final topic related to your self-care: spirituality. This chapter will help you reflect on your spirituality and give you suggestions on how to connect more with yourself, others, and the world around you. Having a deeper connection with yourself and the world will help you get through stressful times and give you a better outlook on your life.

8.1: Spirituality vs. Religion

Some of you who are reading this are not religious. You do not believe in God, follow a particular faith, or have any involvement with a religious denomination. Others who are reading this do believe in God, follow a certain religion, or are deeply involved with a faith. For those of you who are not religious, you might see this chapter and think that nothing will apply to you.

Wrong! Keep reading because everyone can find something valuable in this chapter whether religious or not.

YOUR TURN 8.1

Assessing my Spirituality

Directions: But wait—you may be thinking, "religion and spirituality are the same things, right?" Actually, no! Spirituality and religion are different in many ways. Before we delve into the differences, let's take a brief moment to consider some relevant statements. Read the following statements below and select whether you agree or disagree.

1.	My life means searching and asking	Agree	Disagree
2.	I try to open my mind	Agree	Disagree
3.	I feel deep peace inside of me	Agree	Disagree
4.	I see a friendly world around me	Agree	Disagree
5.	I try to be patient and tolerant	Agree	Disagree
6.	I try to help others	Agree	Disagree
7.	I feel like I have a calling or purpose	Agree	Disagree

What stood out as you went through the statements above? Did you notice any patterns or themes? We sure hope you did because there are some common threads in all of the questions. We will talk more about this later toward the end of this chapter.

Most religions have similar characteristics. First, religion involves practices and rituals that are organized by groups, and they usually occur in public, for example in a church, mosque, or temple. Religion is known as denominational because each religious faith includes distinct traditions. These traditions include worshiping in outward forms such as singing, chanting, or reading scripture. Each religion also holds specific beliefs—these beliefs occur through our thoughts. Finally, those who follow a religious faith engage in a relationship with someone or something outside of themselves. So for example, those who follow Islam have a deep relationship with Allah. Some Native American tribes have relationships with numerous deities represented by spirits of the earth, water, or sky. Keep these words in mind when you think of religion: public, external, and thoughts.

So what is spirituality then? Well, spirituality is harder to define, and there is no set definition. However, spirituality does encompass shared core characteristics. Most people who have a spiritual experience will often keep this experience private. This experience also involves a deep and powerful feeling—usually a feeling of peace, joy, wonder, awe, or bliss. Spiritual experiences often involve emotions. No matter who you are, where you live on the planet, or what you are doing right now, each person has the potential to have a spiritual experience. In other words, these experiences can be spontaneous. Keep these words in mind when you think of spirituality: private, internal, emotions.

Remember the statements you looked over at the beginning of the chapter? Let's take a look at the various themes in those statements and how they relate to spirituality. When we talk about spirituality, there is usually a sense that we are searching for meaning and purpose in our lives. Some of you starting your first year in college may have no idea what you want to do with your career. Other students may know exactly what they want to do professionally and may also have a major selected but later change it to something else. At some point in time, all of you will start reflecting on this important question: "What do I want to do with my life?"

As you go through college, you will be faced with many challenges and obstacles which may leave you feeling confused, afraid, or alone. Spirituality can help you create a sense of inner peace and harmony, help you work through those challenging situations, and give you a sense of hope about your future. You also may feel more connected to people or things around you by engaging in spiritual activities.

Tool Box 8.1

- Spirituality and religion are two different concepts.
- You do not need to be religious to develop your spirituality.
- Spirituality is a private experience that focuses on emotions.

- Spirituality is about finding deeper meanings and purpose in your life, cultivating peace and love within yourself, and developing a connection to the world around you.

Did You Know?

- There is a growing trend among teenagers and young adults who identify as spiritual rather than religious.
- Spirituality has been found to be an important component of wellness in adolescents and young adults.

8.2: Cultivating Your Spirituality

Now that we have talked about what spirituality is, it is time to start helping you work on developing your spirituality. There are many ways to do this, and as we have discussed in other chapters, you should find what works best for you. This may be one of the most challenging components of wellness, but it can also be the most rewarding. So if you find yourself struggling with developing your spirituality, do not be discouraged!

Finding Deeper Meanings

Have you ever felt that you were part of something greater than yourself? Did you ever feel a deep connection to people you were around? Or maybe you had a powerful experience when you were out in nature? Perhaps you felt a deep calling to do something good for others? Or maybe you have struggled to answer that difficult question, "Just who am I?"

Talking about spirituality without talking about meaning and purpose is impossible. What are we talking about when we bring up meaning and purpose? Well, this refers to a sense of direction in life—feeling that you are contributing to the world and moving in a direction that is personally fulfilling. When we talk about meaning or meaningfulness, we are talking about the belief that you can make a choice and, more importantly, that this choice will create the outcome for which you are hoping.

The stronger the sense of meaning and purpose that you have in life, the stronger sense of your identity—helping you answer that difficult question: "Who am I?" And how is this important? If you have a strong sense of yourself, you have more self-esteem. Having more self-esteem is directly related to living a fulfilling life.

Here is something else to consider. When you have a profound sense of meaning and purpose in your life, you are much more likely to feel comfortable in social situations. So you can search out people who have the same values, ideals, and beliefs as you. As a result, your social network grows and you have greater support systems if you go through challenging situations.

YOUR TURN 8.2

Finding Meaning and Purpose

Directions: Try this reflective exercise on meaning and purpose in your own life. Think about a difficult situation you have gone through in the last couple of years. Maybe it was the death of a close family member or beloved pet. Perhaps you broke up with your partner. Maybe you left home to attend college. Pick a situation and answer the following prompts:

Before I went through this experience, I thought of myself as

_____

_____

Now, I see myself as

_____

_____

As I went through this experience, I felt like I could turn to

_____

_____

Looking back on this experience, I feel that this has helped me to

_____

_____

_____

As you go through your college experience, you may find many times when you feel alone, isolated, or a sense of emptiness. You may ask yourself, "Why is this happening to me? What did I do to deserve this?" These are difficult questions and maybe the answer is not right in front of you. All is not lost though. If you have a greater sense of meaning and purpose in your life, you are better able to make sense of those stressful events and have a more positive outlook on what will happen. Think of it this way—if I assign positive meanings to situations, I will experience positive emotions. If I experience positive emotions, I can weather the storms that will inevitably come my direction.

Now you may be thinking, "Well this is all great, but I cannot have a smile on my face 100 percent of the time and feel happy every second." This is true, and you should allow yourself to experience those painful emotions. The key is not to stick with them for too long. Here is why—when you feel these negative emotions for a long time, eventually you will not be able to think clearly, and you will be less likely to work through your problem. Give yourself the time and space to find meaning in difficult situations because as you create these meanings, you will be more likely to experience positive emotions which will help reduce (and even better, get rid of) those negative feelings.

Tool Box 8.2

- Meaning and purpose gives you direction in your life.
- When you have direction, you do not feel so helpless.
- Meaning and purpose can help you understand who you are.
- The more you know about yourself, the greater your chances of dealing positively with stressful situations.

Did You Know?

- Adolescents and young adults with lower levels of spiritual wellness are more likely to experience depression.
- Adolescents who have a strong sense of spirituality are less likely to use drugs or alcohol.
- Adolescents and young adults who develop their spirituality are more likely to see better academic outcomes.

Being in the Moment

Have you ever felt like you were just always so busy with studying or sports that you never had time to stop and breathe? Did you experience moments in your life when you were so worried about a future exam or just kept dwelling on an embarrassing moment with your friends? Or maybe you were driving to a friend's house and realized that 15 minutes went by and you had no idea how you arrived safely because you were not even focused on driving? Well, we all have experienced these moments, and these are the moments that sometimes cause us the most suffering.

Now consider the other moments when you felt as if you were completely in the moment—you did not have one thought about the past or consider anything in the future. How did you remember feeling? Odds are you felt pretty good and this is no coincidence. If you could just learn to be more present, maybe you could experience a greater sense of calm and peace. Well, there happens to be a way to do that and it is called *mindfulness*.

YOUR TURN 8.3

Am I Mindful?

Directions: Before we talk about what mindfulness is, take a moment to reflect on the following statements:

1. I watch my feelings without getting lost in them.

2. I criticize myself for having emotions.

3. It is difficult to stay focused on what is happening in the moment.

4. I notice the colors, shapes, and textures when I am out in nature.

5. I can notice how my emotions influence my thoughts or actions.

Mindfulness has been around for thousands of years. It has only been made popular here in the United States in the last few decades by Jon Kabat-Zinn. Mindfulness is a way of engaging with yourself and the world so you learn to be more present and in the moment. You learn how to detach from your thoughts about the past or the future. Mindfulness also helps you let go of all the self-shaming, self-blaming, or self-critical thoughts you have. You learn how to be mindful through guided exercises and meditations. We will provide some examples later.

You might be wondering, "How does mindfulness help with my spirituality?" Well, at the heart of spirituality is a sense of connectedness to yourself and the world around you. When you feel this sense of connectedness, you begin to feel compassion and kindness towards yourself and others. This deep feeling of compassion is the core of self-care and personal transformation and growth. After all, the meaning of self-care is pretty obvious just by looking at it, right? You are attempting to *care* for your *self*. To do this, you must cultivate a deep connection with who you are and a deep love for yourself.

By letting go of judgments, you free yourself from negativity and open your heart to positivity and love—this is where transformation and growth happens. Think of all the times that you blamed and criticized yourself for not doing well on an exam, not meeting your parents' expectations, or not being able to follow through with a promise to a friend. How much energy did you put into these moments? What were the end results? Chances are you felt stuck, distraught, and discouraged from taking risks. Imagine if you could have gone back to that moment—what would you have told yourself differently? Odds are that message would be one of compassion. Why are you still blaming and criticizing yourself now?

There are additional benefits to developing a mindfulness practice in your own life. You immediately begin to deal with situations in a more relaxed way. As you relax and learn to respond to situations versus reacting on pure emotion, you can to step back and think more clearly. This allows you to make better decisions. As you make better decisions, you experience more positive outcomes which lead to a positive outlook on your life.

Sitting with distressing emotions allows you to explore your experience. You give yourself the opportunity to understand who you are on a deeper level. The more you know yourself, the stronger your self-identity becomes. As you begin to understand yourself, you start noticing your strengths and qualities. This leads to increased self-esteem. The better you feel about yourself, the more likely you are to take risks and challenge yourself in positive ways. These challenges push you out of your comfort zone and you learn to develop deeper meanings about yourself and the world around you. Are you seeing a pattern here?

Figure 8.1

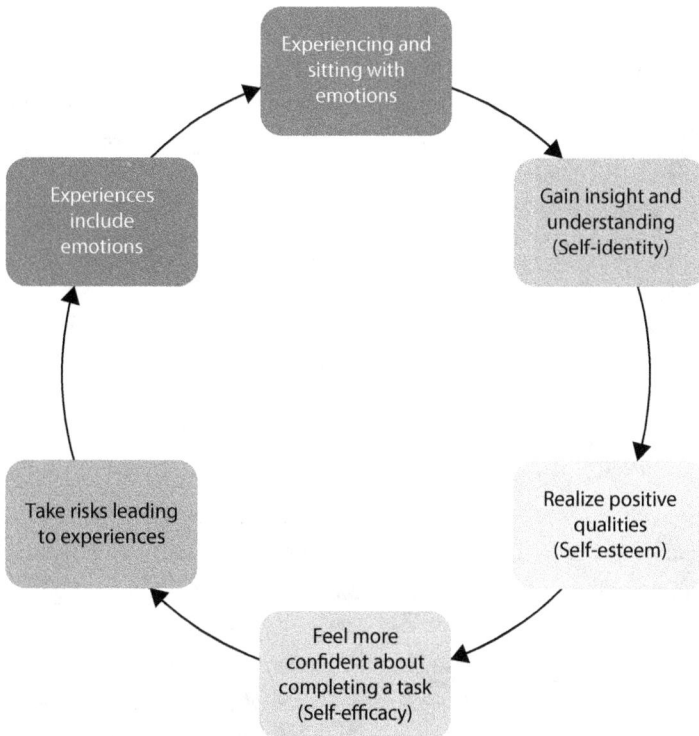

Incorporating mindfulness into your lifestyle will help you feel more empowered to make better decisions. You won't get so caught up in all those negative thoughts that constantly bombard you on a daily basis. Without being so distracted by negativity, you open yourself up to the mysteries of this world and what is occurring all around you. You begin to develop a deeper appreciation and gratitude for the people in your life and what is around you.

Last but certainly not least, mindfulness practice will help you develop a greater sense of intuition. In other words, you can gain more insight into your thoughts and emotions. You have a better understanding of what is truly going on inside of you. This can be incredibly empowering because once you have this understanding, you are then able to take control of your own life. This brings a sense of freedom and inner peace rather than feeling lost, stuck, or out of control.

Let's recap a moment on all the components of spirituality and then we will put it into practice. First, spirituality is an individual experience. This personal experience is usually private and connected to your emotions. The feelings most closely related to spirituality are a feeling of love and connectedness toward yourself and the world around you. These feelings can only be experienced when you remain present and in the moment. When you remain present, you open the door to experience and insight which leads to greater transformation and growth.

YOUR TURN 8.4

Practicing Mindfulness

Directions: Now that you have a greater understanding of mindfulness, let's do an activity to help you practice. This mindfulness activity is called the loving-kindness meditation and it will help you develop the connectedness to yourself and others which we talked about earlier. Before you begin, find a quiet and private place to sit so you will not be distracted or interrupted while doing this exercise.

As you begin this exercise stop and become present. Allow yourself to become aware of your body and mind. Notice what you are experiencing in your body and the thoughts that are running through your mind. Maybe you are thinking about all the reading you have to do, or when you have to attend practice, or thinking about someone you just met at a party or social club.

Just notice and acknowledge what is there without judging or evaluating it. Now, shift your focus to your breath. Let yourself breathe normally and naturally—becoming aware as you breathe in and being aware of breathing out.

Now bring your attention and awareness to your chest and your heart area. Allow yourself to feel any sensations. Let these sensations go where they need to go. Bring your awareness to the beating of your heart and remind yourself that the heart is the window to deeper compassion and love for yourself and the world around you.

It may be difficult to feel this love toward yourself. Just acknowledge this struggle and continue to just discover what it feels like to experience giving this love to yourself.

Now read the following statements and just let yourself sit with them for a few moments:

> *May I be safe.*
> *May I be healthy.*
> *May I be at peace.*

Now think about those who are closest to you—those who you love the most. Repeat the following phrases, filling in the blank space with someone in particular who you would like to expand love and kindness towards:

> *May _____ be safe.*
> *May _____ be healthy.*
> *May_____ be at peace.*

Continue to expand this awareness to someone who has deeply inspired you—perhaps a mentor or teacher—and repeat the phrases again:

> *May _____ be safe.*
> *May _____ be healthy.*
> *May_____ be at peace.*

Bring up people in your life who you would consider an acquaintance or maybe a stranger you passed by on your way to class and repeat the statements:

May they be safe.
May they be healthy.
May they be at peace.

Now bring to mind someone who has hurt you in the past and consider extending this love and kindness to them. This may be difficult or seem impossible but remember that holding on to anger and resentment can be toxic for your well-being. Give yourself this opportunity to begin letting go of that hurt by repeating the following statements:

May _____ be safe.
May _____ be healthy.
May_____ be at peace.

Take a moment to reflect on your experience with this loving-kindness meditation. What did you notice? What thoughts, feelings, or sensations came up for you as you went through this exercise?

We do not have time to review all the different types of mindfulness activities. There are entire books on mindfulness that you can purchase. Below are many other mindfulness activities that you can look into and incorporate into your daily practice:

1. Meditation
2. Deep-breathing exercises
3. Mindful walking
4. Mindful eating
5. Silent retreats
6. Body scan

Tool Box 8.3

- Find opportunities to be in the moment.
- Use mindfulness activities to help you live moment to moment.

- Open yourself up to painful emotions and experiences.
- Let go of judgment and self-critical thoughts.

Time Alone

One of the greatest hurdles to developing your spirituality is finding time for yourself. Think of everything you have to accomplish on a given day. You may think, "I have to go to class, work at my job, go to my student government meeting, work on my research paper, and study for my exam—and all in one day! How am I going to have enough time to get everything done?" Along with checking off your day-to-day activities, you may also find yourself getting attached to another barrier to spirituality—technology.

Technology has grown so fast in the past 20 years. Just think about what has changed since you were a child. We are more connected to each other than we have ever been in history. Gone are the days when you had to wait weeks to hear back from someone. You can now send a message in an instant to a friend across the world. Think of all the gadgets that you use on a daily basis—your cell phone, car GPS, iPad, computer, tablet, and so forth. Technology has made it easier to connect with one another and have access to information as soon as it becomes available.

You can practically do everything online now—you can shop for textbooks, access research articles, attend classes, find social clubs to attend on campus, or even form online study groups so you do not have to leave home. Social media has also had a dramatic effect on how we stay connected with one another. There are digital apps that help you manage almost every aspect of your day-to-day life. Technology has changed the way we interact with the world and each other. But has this all been a positive change or has this come at a cost?

YOUR TURN 8.5

Am I Too Plugged In?

Directions: Let's do a small exercise and see just how much you are plugged into technology. Review each item and write down how much time you spend using each item on a daily basis.

Item		Time Spent on Daily Use
Television		_____
Computer:	Desktop	_____
	Laptop	_____
Phone:	Texting	_____
	Talking	_____
Tablet/iPad		_____
Social Media:	Facebook	_____
	Twitter	_____
	YouTube	_____
	Other	_____
Total Hours		_____

Here is a recommendation—keep a log, or media diary, for five days and write down each time your eyes are in front of some screen and for how much time.

So what do you notice? Chances are, if you are like most young adults, you are spending a lot of time tethered to technology or social media. Although there are many benefits to staying connected with others and making our lives easier through apps, we also lose connection to the world around us. We become so hyper-focused on how many messages we receive from friends or family or on all the tasks we have to complete in such a short period that we forget to stop, take a moment, and enjoy what is around us. We fail to remember the benefits of time alone with ourselves.

After all, how can you take a moment to explore your identity and what is meaningful to you if you do not even give yourself that moment? To take time, you have to make time. But we understand—finding that time when you have classes to attend, studying, social clubs or sports, or a job can seem impossible. Unfortunately, you do not have super powers and eventually your emotional, psychological, and spiritual batteries run out. You have to find time to unplug from technology and recharge those batteries.

The question is, how do you find the balance between meeting the demands of life through technology while also finding time to find peace and fulfillment? Here are some ideas that we recommend.

You probably spend your morning planning out everything you have to do. So why not plan to include some unplugging time? Schedule some time out in your day when you turn everything off. You do not even have to unplug for a long time—even taking 20 minutes out of your day will have tremendous health benefits.

Complete a list of activities or hobbies that you enjoy doing which do not include your cell phone, computer, or TV. When you feel tempted to look at the screen, pull out this list and do one of those activities.

At least once every few months, schedule a tech detox weekend. You can do this by yourself or get a group of friends to participate. Plan a weekend trip where you can get away from your day-to-day environment and set a strict "no tech" policy—your cell phones stay off and you do not check emails or read on your tablet. You can even participate in silent retreats specifically designed to help you disconnect from technology and reconnect with yourself.

Ever hear the saying "fight fire with fire?" Well, use technology against itself to unplug. You can download apps on your phone that will help block access to social media programs for certain periods of time. This will allow you to find other alternatives to spending time that do not involve technology. Perhaps this would be a perfect opportunity to try one of those mindfulness activities!

Did You Know?

- 92 percent of adolescents use their smartphones to go online daily.
- 71 percent of adolescents use more than one social network site.
- On average, adolescents and young adults send and receive around 30 text messages per day.

Tool Box 8.4

- Be mindful of how much you use technology and social media.
- Take time to unplug from technology.
- Make time for other activities that are fulfilling to you.

The Hand in the Dark

Adjusting to college life can be hard and lonely. I moved from a small town in Idaho to Chicago and could not get over the culture shock. Everything was so different for me. I had never lived in a big city before, and I'd never been around so many people. Instead of endless fields of corn and farms, there were towering structures of metal. The peace and serenity of quiet, starlit evenings were replaced with sirens, horns, and construction.

I was able to keep in touch with friends and family back home through Facebook and Skype. Somehow, I still felt disconnected from everyone—including myself. Slowly, I started to withdraw from everything and everyone. I wasn't making phone calls back home as often or replying to text messages. I remember struggling to get out of bed and go to class. Even the smallest tasks seemed like huge struggles. I remember thinking, "Did I make the right choice to come here?" My roommate, Li, started to become really worried about me. Li was an international student and had moved to Chicago a few years ago from China.

Then one day Li stormed into my room and practically dragged me out of bed. She told me she was taking me to a meditation class. "This has to stop! You're not doing yourself any favors by staying in this room—trust me. I have been down this road." I was shocked to hear those words. I always saw Li as so put together and having everything in place in her life the way she wanted it. This little spark of curiosity gave me a glimmer of hope so I decided to go.

We arrived at the wellness center on campus. Li showed me to the room where we would be meditating. I had never meditated before and was terrified of what might happen. I was never really good with dealing with the unknown and this was completely out of my comfort zone. The instructor greeted us and we all were instructed to take our places and sit down on our meditation mats. The instructor began leading us through a guided meditation—she used guided imagery to help create scenes and images in our mind.

Not too long into the meditation, I immediately felt a rush of fear and panic. I remember seeing images of home all around me and then a door would shut in front of each image until nothing else was left but darkness. I was alone again. I wanted to run from this feeling. I wanted to stuff it down and shove it far away but I stayed with these feelings.

Then something occurred which I can only describe as spiritual. In the darkness, I felt that there was someone with me. I can remember feeling like someone was gently grabbing my hand and then I heard someone say, "You're just scared, Jen. Everything will be okay. You will find your way. Let's just take this one step at a time, okay?" The voice was all too familiar—it was mine! It was like this other version of me from another part of reality but a version that I could see myself becoming.

Afterward, Li and I went out together for dinner. I told her about my spiritual experience and she told me all about how she had a similar experience. Li told me about how lost and alone she felt when she first moved to the city. I realized through our conversation that I had been running from these feelings which were making me feel disconnected from everything and lost.

That moment was a life-changing experience for me. I realized so many things about myself and finally felt like I understood what was going on. I remember feeling like I had control of my life again. Soon after, I found myself taking more risks. I was able to go to classes and even joined a social club on campus. Li took me out a lot and introduced me to her friends. I started feeling that same connection that I had back home. Each day I woke up, I felt like I was moving towards a goal and I started feeling more confident about myself. I started talking more with my family and friends back home and they even said that they could notice a difference in me. Everything was starting to come together.

Fast forward a year and I am still going to that meditation class. I find it helpful to keep making time to sit with myself and understand what is going on internally. I always learn more about myself. Ironically, I feel like I have learned more about myself in that last year than ever before. I also feel more positive about my life and connected to people. Even my relationships with family members back home have grown stronger. So my advice to all who are reading is to find ways to spend time with yourself and get to know how you are. Take the time to explore what is holding you back and surround yourself with people who care. If you are experiencing what I went through, please know that it gets better, but you have to be active in changing your life.

REFERENCES

Aida, H., Heather, G., Maria, V., & Peter, W. (2013). Diabetes awareness and behavioural risk factors among university students in Saudi Arabia. *Middle East Journal of Family Medicine, 11*(3), 4–9.

American Psychiatric Association. (2013). *Diagnostic and Statistical Manual of Mental Disorders* (5th ed.). Arlington, VA: American Psychiatric Publishing.

Amuta, A. O., & Barry, A. E. (2015). Type 2 diabetes family history and engagement in protective nutrition behaviors: A cross-sectional study of college students. *American Journal of Health Studies, 30*(3), 135–145.

Artime, T. M., & Buchholz, K. R. (2016). Treatment for sexual assault survivors at university counseling centers. *Journal of College Student Psychotherapy, 30*(4), 252. doi:10.1080/87568225.2016.1219610

Awang, M. M., Kutty, F. M., & Ahmad, A. R. (2014). Perceived social support and well being: First-year student experience in university. *International Education Studies, 7*(13), 261–270.

Ažic, S. S., & Antulic, S. (2013). Adjustment to college and the student mentoring programme. *Croatian Journal Educational/Hrvatski Casopis Za Odgoj I Obrazovanje, 15*(3), 715–740.

Azizi, M., Aghaee, N., Ebrahimi, M., & Ranjbar, K. (2011). Nutrition knowledge, the attitude and practices of college students. *Facta Universitatis: Series Physical Education & Sport, 9*(3), 349–357.

Balfe, M. (2007). Alcohol, diabetes and the student body. *Health, Risk & Society, 9*(3), 241–257. doi:10.1080/13698570701488951

Barbosa Felipe, A. O., Pimenta Carvalho, A. M., & Baptista Andrade, C. U. (2015). Spirituality and religion as protectors for adolescent drug use. *SMAD Revista Electronica Salud Mental, Alcohol y Drogas, 11*(1), 49–58. doi:10.11606/issn.1806-6976.v11i1p49-58

Barkley, J. E., & Lepp, A. (2016). Mobile phone use among college students is a sedentary leisure behavior which may interfere with exercise. *Computers in Human Behavior, 56,* 29–33. doi:10.1016/j.chb.2015.11.001

Baruch-Runyon, A., VanZandt, Z., & Elliott, S. A. (2009). Forging connections: An investigation of new students' perspectives of their transition to the university. *NACADA Journal, 29*(1), 31–42.

Bedera, N., & Nordmeyer, K. (2015). 'Never go out alone': An analysis of college rape prevention tips. *Sexuality & Culture, 19*(3), 533–542. doi:10.1007/s12119-015-9274-5

Benton, S. A., Heesacker, M., Snowden, S. J., & Lee, G. (2016). Therapist-assisted, online (TAO) intervention for anxiety in college students: TAO outperformed treatment as usual. *Professional Psychology: Research & Practice, 47*(5), 363–371. doi:10.1037/pro0000097

Berenz, E. C., Kevorkian, S., Chowdhury, N., Dick, D. M., Kendler, K. S., & Amstadter, A. B. (2016). Posttraumatic stress disorder symptoms, anxiety sensitivity, and alcohol-use motives in college students with a history of interpersonal trauma. *Psychology of Addictive Behaviors: Journal of the Society of Psychologists in Addictive Behaviors, 30*(7), 755–763.

Bernstein, C., & Chemaly, C. (2016). Sex role identity and academic stress and wellbeing of first-year university students. *Gender & Behaviour, 14*(3), 7547–7573.

Besser, A., & Zeigler-Hill, V. (2014). Positive personality features and stress among first-year university students: Implications for psychological distress, functional impairment, and self-esteem. *Self & Identity, 13*(1), 24–44. doi:10.1080/15298 868.2012.736690

Blair, A. (2017). Understanding first-year students' transition to university: A pilot study with implications for student engagement, assessment, and feedback. *Politics, 37*(2), 215–228. doi:10.1177/0263395716633904

Bliton, C. F., Wolford-Clevenger, C., Zapor, H., Elmquist, J., Brem, M. J., Shorey, R. C., & Stuart, G. L. (2016). Emotion dysregulation, gender, and intimate partner violence perpetration: An exploratory study in college students. *Journal of Family Violence, 31*(3), 371–377. doi:10.1007/s10896-015-9772-0

Boehm, M. A., Lei, Q. M., Lloyd, R. M., & Prichard, J. R. (2016). Depression, anxiety, and tobacco use: Overlapping impediments to sleep in a national sample of college students. *Journal of American College Health, 64*(7), 565–574. doi:10.1 080/07448481.2016.1205073

Briggs, M. K., & Shoffner, M. F. (2006). Spiritual wellness and depression: Testing a theoretical model with older adolescents and midlife adults. *Counseling and Values, 51*(1), 5.

Briggs, M. K., Akos, P., Czyszczon, G., & Eldridge, A. (2011). Assessing and promoting spiritual wellness as a protective factor in secondary schools. *Counseling & Values, 55*(2), 171–184.

Brooman, S., & Darwent, S. (2014). Measuring the beginning: A quantitative study of the transition to higher education. *Studies in Higher Education, 39*(9), 1523–1541. doi:10.1080/03075079.2013.801428

Brown, M. V., Flint, M., & Fuqua, J. (2014). The effects of a nutrition education intervention on vending machine sales on a university campus. *Journal of American College Health: J of ACH, 62*(7), 512–516. doi:10.1080/07448481.2014.920337

Brown, O. N., O'Connor, L. E., & Savaiano, D. (2014). Mobile MyPlate: A pilot study using text messaging to provide nutrition education and promote better dietary choices in college students. *Journal of American College Health: J of ACH, 62*(5), 320–327. doi:10.1080/07448481.2014.899233

Buhi, E. R., Marhefka, S. L., Wheldon, C. W., Tilley, D. L., Klinkenberger, N., Lescano, C., & Hoban, M. T. (2014). Sexual and reproductive health disparities in a national sample of Hispanic and non-Hispanic white U.S. college students. *Journal of Health Disparities Research & Practice, 7*(1), 19–36.

Burnett, A. J., Sabato, T. M., Wagner, L., & Smith, A. (2014). The influence of attributional style on substance use and risky sexual behavior among college students. *College Student Journal, 48*(2), 325–336.

Bussing, A., Foller-Mancini, A., Gidley, J., & Heusser, P. (2010). Aspects of spirituality in adolescents. *International Journal of Children's Spirituality, 15*(1), 25–44. doi:10.1080/13644360903565524

Champion, D. A., Lewis, T. F., & Myers, J. E. (2015). College student alcohol use and abuse: Social norms, health beliefs, and selected socio-demographic variables as explanatory factors. *Journal of Alcohol and Drug Education, 59*(1), 57–82.

Chang, E. C., Lian, X., Yu, T., Qu, J., Zhang, B., Jia, W., . . . Hirsch, J. K. (2015). Loneliness under assault: Understanding the impact of sexual assault on the relation between loneliness and suicidal risk in college students. *Personality and Individual Differences, 72*, 155–159. doi:10.1016/j.paid.2014.09.001

Chang, L. (2014). College students' search for sexual health information from their best friends: An application of the theory of motivated information management. *Asian Journal of Social Psychology, 17*(3), 196–205. doi:10.1111/ajsp.12063

Christoph, M. J., Ellison, B. D., & Meador, E. N. (2016). The influence of nutrition label placement on awareness and use among college students in a dining hall setting. *Journal of the Academy of Nutrition & Dietetics, 116*(9), 1395–1405. doi:10.1016/j.jand.2016.05.003

Bum, C., & Jeon, I. (2016). Structural relationships between students' social support and self-esteem, depression, and happiness. *Social Behavior & Personality: An International Journal, 44*(11), 1761–1774. doi:10.2224/sbp.2016.44.11.1761

Cil Akinci, A., Yildiz, H., & Zengin, N. (2011). The level of comfort among nursing students during sexual counseling to patients who have chronic medical conditions. *Sexuality & Disability, 29*(1), 11–20. doi:10.1007/s11195-010-9185-1

Çivitci, A. (2015). The moderating role of positive and negative affect on the relationship between perceived social support and stress in college students. *Educational Sciences: Theory & Practice, 15*(3), 565–573. doi:10.12738/estp.2015.3.2553

Collison, D., Banbury, S., & Lusher, J. (2016). Relationships between age, sex, self-esteem and attitudes towards alcohol use amongst university students. *Journal of Alcohol & Drug Education, 60*(2), 16–34.

Concepcion, T., Barbosa, C., Vélez, J. C., Pepper, M., Andrade, A., Gelaye, B., ... Williams, M. A. (2014). Daytime sleepiness, poor sleep quality, eveningness chronotype, and common mental disorders among Chilean college students. *Journal of American College Health, 62*(7), 441–448. doi:10.1080/07448481.2014.917652

Conley, A. H., Overstreet, C. M., Hawn, S. E., Kendler, K. S., Dick, D. M., & Amstadter, A. B. (2017). Prevalence and predictors of sexual assault among a college sample. *Journal of American College Health: J of ACH, 65*(1), 41–49. doi:10.1080/07448481.2016.1235578

Conley, C. S., Travers, L. V., & Bryant, F. B. (2013). Promoting psychosocial adjustment and stress management in first-year college students: The benefits of engagement in a psychosocial wellness seminar. *Journal of American College Health, 61*(2), 75–86.

Czyz, E. K., Horwitz, A. G., Eisenberg, D., Kramer, A., & King, C. A. (2013). Self-reported barriers to professional help seeking among college students at elevated risk for suicide. *Journal of American College Health: J of ACH, 61*(7), 398–406. doi:10.1080/07448481.2013.820731

Dawson, M., & Pooley, J. A. (2013). Resilience: The role of optimism, perceived parental autonomy support and perceived social support in first year university students. *Journal of Education and Training Studies, 1*(2), 38–49.

de Vries, J. D., van Hooff, M. L. M., Geurts, S. A. E., & Kompier, M. A. J. (2016). Exercise as an intervention to reduce study-related fatigue among university students: A two-arm parallel randomized controlled trial. *Plos One, 11*(3), e0152137-e0152137. doi:10.1371/journal.pone.0152137

Dinh, K. T., Holmberg, M. D., Ho, I. K., & Haynes, M. C. (2014). The relationship of prejudicial attitudes to psychological, social, and physical well-being within a sample of college students in the United States. *Journal of Cultural Diversity, 21*(2), 56–66.

Druckman, J. N., Gilli, M., Klar, S., & Robison, J. (2015). Measuring drug and alcohol use among college student-athletes. *Social Science Quarterly (Wiley-Blackwell), 96*(2), 369–380. doi:10.1111/ssqu.12135

Dvorak, R. D., Lamis, D. A., & Malone, P. S. (2013). Alcohol use, depressive symptoms, and impulsivity as risk factors for suicide proneness among college students. *Journal of Affective Disorders, 149*(1–3), 326–334. doi:10.1016/j.jad.2013.01.046

Dvořáková, K., Kishida, M., Li, J., Elavsky, S., Broderick, P. C., Agrusti, M. R., & Greenberg, M. T. (2017). Promoting healthy transition to college through mindfulness training with first-year college students: Pilot randomized controlled trial. *Journal of American College Health, 65*(4), 259–267. doi:10.1080/07448481.2017.1278605

Economos, C. D., Hildebrandt, M. L., & Hyatt, R. R. (2008). College freshman stress and weight change: Differences by gender. *American Journal of Health Behavior, 32*(1), 16–25.

Edman, J. L., Lynch, W. C., & Yates, A. (2014). The impact of exercise performance dissatisfaction and physical exercise on symptoms of depression among college students: A gender comparison. *The Journal of Psychology, 148*(1), 23–35.

Edwards, K. M., Littleton, H. L., Sylaska, K. M., Crossman, A. L., & Craig, M. (2016). College campus community readiness to address intimate partner violence among LGBTQ+ young adults: A conceptual and empirical examination. *American Journal of Community Psychology, 58*(1–2), 16–26. doi:10.1002/ajcp.12068

Edwards, K. M., & Sylaska, K. M. (2013). The perpetration of intimate partner violence among LGBTQ college youth: The role of minority stress. *Journal of Youth and Adolescence, 42*(11), 1721–1731. doi:10.1007/s10964-012-9880-6

Eisenbarth, C. (2012). Does self-esteem moderate the relations among perceived stress, coping, and depression? *College Student Journal, 46*(1), 149–157.

Feng, B., & Magen, E. (2016). Relationship closeness predicts unsolicited advice giving in supportive interactions. *Journal of Social & Personal Relationships, 33*(6), 751–767. doi:10.1177/0265407515592262

Field, C. J., Kimuna, S. R., & Lang, M. N. (2015). The relation of interracial relationships to intimate partner violence by college students. *Journal of Black Studies, 46*(4), 384–403. doi:10.1177/0021934715574804

Frey, L. L., Beesley, D., Hurst, R., Saldana, S., & Licuanan, B. (2016). Instrumentality, expressivity, and relational qualities in the same-sex friendships of college women and men. *Journal of College Counseling, 19*(1), 17–30. doi:10.1002/jocc.12028

Fuertes, J. N., & Hoffman, A. (2016). Alcohol consumption and abuse among college students: Alarming rates among the best and the brightest. *College Student Journal, 50*(2), 236–240.

Garcia, C. M., Lechner, K. E., Frerich, E. A., Lust, K. A., & Eisenberg, M. E. (2014). College students' preferences for health care providers when accessing sexual health resources. *Public Health Nursing, 31*(5), 387–394. doi:10.1111/phn.12121

Gaultney, J. F. (2016). Risk for sleep disorder measured during students' first college semester may predict institutional retention and grade point average over a 3-year period, with indirect effects through self-efficacy. *Journal of College Student Retention: Research, Theory & Practice, 18*(3), 333–359. doi:10.1177/1521025115622784

Geng, G., & Midford, R. (2015). Investigating first year education students' stress level. *Australian Journal of Teacher Education, 40*(6), 1–12.

Giordano, A. L., & Cashwell, C. S. (2014). Exploring the relationship between social interest, social bonding, and collegiate substance abuse. *Journal of College Counseling, 17*(3), 222–235. doi:10.1002/j.2161-1882.2014.00059.x

Goldstein, S. B. (2013). Predicting college students' intergroup friendships across race/ethnicity, religion, sexual orientation, and social class. *Equity & Excellence in Education, 46*(4), 502–519.

Granello, P. (2013). *Wellness counseling.* Boston, MA: Pearson Higher Education.

Gray, R., Vitak, J., Easton, E. W., & Ellison, N. B. (2013). Examining social adjustment to college in the age of social media: Factors influencing successful transitions and persistence. *Computers & Education, 67*, 193–207. doi:10.1016/j.compedu.2013.02.021

Haardörfer, R., Berg, C. J., Lewis, M., Payne, J., Pillai, D., McDonald, B., & Windle, M. (2016). Polytobacco, marijuana, and alcohol use patterns in college students: A latent class analysis. *Addictive Behaviors, 59*, 58–64. doi:10.1016/j.addbeh.2016.03.034

Hagman, B. T., Cohn, A. M., Schonfeld, L., Moore, K., & Barrett, B. (2014). College students who endorse a sub-threshold number of DSM-5 alcohol use disorder criteria: Alcohol, tobacco, and illicit drug use in DSM-5 diagnostic orphans. *The American Journal on Addictions, 23*(4), 378–385. doi:10.1111/j.1521-0391.2014.12120.x

Hermon, D. A., & Davis, G. A. (2004). College student wellness: A comparison between traditional- and nontraditional-age students. *Journal of College Counseling, 7*(1), 32–39.

Holliday, R., Anderson, E., Williams, R., Bird, J., Matlock, A., Ali, S., . . . Surís, A. (2016). A pilot examination of differences in college adjustment stressors and depression and anxiety symptoms between white, Hispanic and white, non-Hispanic female college students. *Journal of Hispanic Higher Education, 15*(3), 277–288. doi:10.1177/1538192715607331

Hubbs, A., Doyle, E. I., Bowden, R. G., & Doyle, R. D. (2012). Relationships among self-esteem, stress, and physical activity in college students. *Psychological Reports, 110*(2), 469–474. doi:10.2466/02.07.09.PR0.110.2.469-474

Huculak, S., & McLennan, J. D. (2010). "The lord is my shepherd": Examining spirituality as a protection against mental health problems in youth exposed to violence in Brazil. *Mental Health, Religion & Culture, 13*(5), 467–484. doi:10.1080/13674670903406096

Jacobson, L., Daire, A. P., & Abel, E. M. (2015). Intimate partner violence: Implications for counseling self-identified LGBTQ college students engaged in same-sex relationships. *Journal of LGBT Issues in Counseling, 9*(2), 118–135. doi:10.108 0/15538605.2015.1029203

Jiang, W., Huang, Y., & Chen, G. (2012). How cooperativeness and competitiveness influence student burnout: The moderating effect of neuroticism. *Social Behavior & Personality: An International Journal, 40*(5), 805–813.

Jiao, Y., Sun, I. Y., Farmer, A. K., & Lin, K. (2016). College students' definitions of intimate partner violence: A comparative study of three Chinese societies. *Journal of Interpersonal Violence, 31*(7), 1208–1229. doi:10.1177/0886260514564162

Johnson, L. M., Matthews, T. L., & Napper, S. L. (2016). Sexual orientation and sexual assault victimization among US college students. *The Social Science Journal, 53*(2), 174–183. doi:10.1016/j.soscij.2016.02.007

Johnston, L. B., & Stewart, C. (2011). Rethinking GLBTQ adolescent spirituality: Implications for social workers in the twenty-first century. *Journal of GLBT Family Studies, 7*(4), 388–397. doi:10.1080/1550428X.2011.592967

Jozkowski, K. N., & Peterson, Z. D. (2013). College students and sexual consent: Unique insights. *Journal of Sex Research, 50*(6), 517–523. doi:10.1080/00224 499.2012.700739

Kadam, Y. R., Patil, S. R., Waghachavare, V., & Gore, A. D. (2016). Influence of various lifestyle and psychosocial factors on sleep disturbances among the college students: A cross-sectional study from an urban area of India. *Journal of Krishna Institute of Medical Sciences, 5*(3), 51–60.

Kapikiran, S., & Acun-Kapikiran, N. (2016). Optimism and psychological resilience in relation to depressive symptoms in university students: Examining the mediating role of self-esteem. *Educational Sciences: Theory & Practice, 16*(6), 2087–2110. doi:10.12738/estp.2016.6.0107

Kenney, S. R., Paves, A. P., Grimaldi, E. M., & LaBrie, J. W. (2014). Sleep quality and alcohol risk in college students: Examining the moderating effects of drinking motives. *Journal of American College Health: J of ACH, 62*(5), 301–308. doi:10. 1080/07448481.2014.897953

Kerr, D. L., Ding, K., & Chaya, J. (2014). Substance use of lesbian, gay, bisexual and heterosexual college students. *American Journal of Health Behavior, 38*(6), 951–962. doi:10.5993/AJHB.38.6.17

King, K., Vidourek, R., & Singh, A. (2014). Condoms, sex, and sexually transmitted diseases: Exploring sexual health issues among Asian-Indian college students. *Sexuality & Culture, 18*(3), 649–663. doi:10.1007/s12119-013-9214-1

King, K. M., Ling, J., Ridner, L., Jacks, D., Newton, K. S., & Topp, R. (2013). Fit into college II: Physical activity and nutrition behavior effectiveness and programming recommendations. *Recreational Sports Journal, 37*(1), 29–41.

Kirsch, A. C., Conley, C. S., & Riley, T. J. (2015). Comparing psychosocial adjustment across the college transition in a matched heterosexual and lesbian, gay, and bisexual sample. *Journal of College Student Development, 56*(2), 155–169.

Kito, M. (2005). Self-disclosure in romantic relationships and friendships among American and Japanese college students. *The Journal of Social Psychology, 145*(2), 127-140.

Klaw, E. L., Demers, A. L., & Da Silva, N. (2016). Predicting risk factors for intimate partner violence among post-9/11 college student veterans. *Journal of Interpersonal Violence, 31*(4), 572-597. doi:10.1177/0886260514556102

Kotzé, M., & Kleynhans, R. (2013). Psychological well-being and resilience as predictors of first-year students' academic performance. *Journal of Psychology in Africa, 23*(1), 51-59.

Kurt, D. G. (2015). Suicide risk in college students: The effects of Internet addiction and drug use. *Educational Sciences: Theory & Practice, 15*(4), 841-848. doi:10.12738/estp.2015.4.2639

LaFountaine, J., Neisen, M., & Parsons, R. (2006). Wellness factors in first-year college students. *American Journal of Health Studies, 21*(3), 214-218.

Lechner, K. E., Garcia, C. M., Frerich, E. A., Lust, K., & Eisenberg, M. E. (2013). College students' sexual health: Personal responsibility or the responsibility of the college? *Journal of American College Health, 61*(1), 28-35. doi:10.1080/07448481.2012.750608

Lemly, D. C., Lawlor, K., Scherer, E. A., Kelemen, S., & Weitzman, E. R. (2014). College health service capacity to support youth with chronic medical conditions. *Pediatrics, 134*(5), 885-891. doi:10.1542/peds.2014-1304

Lemoyne, J., Valois, P., & Wittman, W. (2016). Analyzing exercise behaviors during the college years: Results from latent growth curve analysis. *Plos One, 11*(4), e0154377-e0154377. doi:10.1371/journal.pone.0154377

Leong, P. (2015). Coming to America: Assessing the patterns of acculturation, friendship formation, and the academic experiences of international students at a U.S. college. *Journal of International Students, 5*(4), 459-474.

Lev Ari, L., & Shulman, S. (2012). Pathways of sleep, affect, and stress constellations during the first year of college: Transition difficulties of emerging adults. *Journal of Youth Studies, 15*(3), 273-292. doi:10.1080/13676261.2011.635196

Lévesque, S., Rodrigue, C., Beaulieu-Prévost, D., Blais, M., Boislard, M., & Lévy, J. J. (2016). Intimate partner violence, sexual assault, and reproductive health among university women. *Canadian Journal of Human Sexuality, 25*(1), 9-20. doi:10.3138/cjhs.251-A5

Lewis, T. F., & Myers, J. E. (2010). Wellness factors as predictors of alcohol use among undergraduates: Implications for prevention and intervention. *Journal of College Counseling, 13*(2), 111-125.

Lewis, T. F., & Myers, J. E. (2010). Wellness Factors as Predictors of Alcohol Use Among Undergraduates. *Journal of College Counseling, 13*, 111-125.

Li, M. (2016). Investigation and analysis on outdoor sports and dietary nutrition of college students. *Carpathian Journal of Food Science & Technology, 8*(3), 160-167.

Lin, K., Sun, I., Wu, Y., & Liu, J. (2016). College students' attitudes toward intimate partner violence: A comparative study of China and the U.S. *Journal of Family Violence, 31*(2), 179-189. doi:10.1007/s10896-015-9759-x

Lindsey, C. (2014). Trait anxiety in college students: The role of the approval seeking schema and separation individuation. *College Student Journal, 48*(3), 407-418.

Lipton, M., Weeks, J., Daruwala, S., & De, L. R. (2016). Profiles of social anxiety and impulsivity among college students: A close examination of profile differences in externalizing behavior. *Journal of Psychopathology & Behavioral Assessment, 38*(3), 465–475. doi:10.1007/s10862-015-9531-9

Lubker, J. R., & Etzel, E. F. (2007). College adjustment experiences of first-year students: Disengaged athletes, nonathletes, and current varsity athletes. *National Association of Student Personnel Administrators, 44*(3), 457–480.

Mahmoud, J. S. R., Staten, R. T., Lennie, T. A., & Hall, L. A. (2015). The relationships of coping, negative thinking, life satisfaction, social support, and selected demographics with anxiety of young adult college students. *Journal of Child and Adolescent Psychiatric Nursing: Official Publication of the Association of Child and Adolescent Psychiatric Nurses, Inc, 28*(2), 97–108. doi:10.1111/jcap.12109

Marr, J., & Wilcox, S. (2015). Self-efficacy and social support mediate the relationship between internal health locus of control and health behaviors in college students. *American Journal of Health Education, 46*(3), 122–131.

Martin, N. D., Tobin, W., & Spenner, K. I. (2014). Interracial friendships across the college years: Evidence from a longitudinal case study. *Journal of College Student Development, 55*(7), 720–725. doi:10.1353/csd.2014.0075

Mason, M. J., Zaharakis, N., & Benotsch, E. G. (2014). Social networks, substance use, and mental health in college students. *Journal of American College Health, 62*(7), 470–477. doi:10.1080/07448481.2014.923428

Mayfield, K., Tang, L., & Bosselman, R. (2014). Nutrition labeling for restaurant menu items: College students' preferences for nutrition information and its influence on purchase intention. *Journal of Quality Assurance in Hospitality & Tourism, 15*(3), 310–325. doi:10.1080/1528008X.2014.921775

McNeely, A. R. (2011). *Differences among community college students on dimensions of wellness as measured by the 5F-Wel-A* . Capella University.

Melander, L. A. (2010). College students' perceptions of intimate partner cyber harassment. *Cyberpsychology, Behavior and Social Networking, 13*(3), 263–268.

Menon, J. A., Mwaba, S. O. C., & Ngoma, M. P. S. (2014). Gearing up for the future—life skills to address sexual and reproductive health in young people. *Medical Journal of Zambia, 41*(3), 145–148.

Merianos, A. L., Nabors, L. A., Vidourek, R. A., & King, K. A. (2013). The impact of self-esteem and social support on college students' mental health. *American Journal of Health Studies, 28*(1), 27–34.

Miller, M. B., DiBello, A. M., Lust, S. A., Carey, M. P., & Carey, K. B. (2016). Adequate sleep moderates the prospective association between alcohol use and consequences. *Addictive Behaviors, 63*, 23–28. doi:10.1016/j.addbeh.2016.05.005

Milojevich, H. M., & Lukowski, A. F. (2016). Sleep and mental health in undergraduate students with generally healthy sleep habits. *Plos One, 11*(6), e0156372-e0156372. doi:10.1371/journal.pone.0156372

Monteiro, A. C., Jeremic, M., & Budden, M. C. (2010). Can we have fries with that, please? Nutrition and physical activities among college students. *Contemporary Issues in Education Research, 3*(11), 1–10.

Moore, E. W., & Smith, W. E. (2012). What college students do not know: Where are the gaps in sexual health knowledge? *Journal of American College Health: J of ACH, 60*(6), 436–442. doi:10.1080/07448481.2012.673521

Moure-Rodríguez, L., Piñeiro, M., Corral Varela, M., Rodríguez-Holguín, S., Cadaveira, F., & Caamaño-Isorna, F. (2016). Identifying predictors and prevalence of alcohol consumption among university students: Nine years of follow-up. *Plos One*, *11*(11), 1-15. doi:10.1371/journal.pone.0165514

Murdock, K. K. (2013). Texting while stressed: Implications for students' burnout, sleep, and well-being. *Psychology of Popular Media Culture*, *2*(4), 207-221. doi:10.1037/ppm0000012

Myers, J. E., Clarke, P., Brown, J. B., & Champion, D. A. (2012). Wellness: Theory, research, and applications for counselors. In M. B. Scholl, A. S. McGowan, & J. T. Hansen (Eds.), *Humanistic perspectives on contemporary counseling issues* (pp. 17-44). New York, NY: Routledge/Taylor & Francis Group.

Myers, J. E., Luecht, R. M., & Sweeney, T. J. (2004). The factor structure of well-ness: Reexamining theoretical and empirical models underlying the wellness evaluation of lifestyle (WEL) and the five-factor wel. *Measurement & Evaluation in Counseling & Development (American Counseling Association)*, *36*(4), 194-208.

Myers, J. E., & Mobley, A. K. (2004). Wellness of undergraduates: Comparisons of tra-ditional and nontraditional students. *Journal of College Counseling*, *7*(1), 40.

Myers, J. E., & Sweeney, T. J. (2004). The indivisible self: An evidence-based model of wellness. *Journal of Individual Psychology*, *60*(3), 234-244.

Myers, J. E., Sweeney, T. J., & Witmer, J. M. (2000). The wheel of wellness counseling for wellness: A holistic model for treatment planning. *Journal of Counseling & Development*, *78*(3), 251-266.

Myers, J. E., Willse, J. T., & Villalba, J. A. (2011). Promoting self-esteem in adoles-cents: The influence of wellness factors. *Journal of Counseling & Development*, *89*(1), 28-36.

National Sleep Foundation (2017). *Sleep hygiene*. Retrieved from https://sleepfoun-dation.org/sleep-topics/sleep-hygiene

Ndasauka, Y., Hou, J., Wang, Y., Yang, L., Yang, Z., Ye, Z., . . . Zhang, X. (2016). Excessive use of Twitter among college students in the UK: Validation of the mi-croblog excessive use scale and relationship to social interaction and loneliness. *Computers in Human Behavior*, *55*, 963-971. doi:10.1016/j.chb.2015.10.020

O'Boyle, N. (2014). Front row friendships: Relational dialectics and identity nego-tiations by mature students at university. *Communication Education*, *63*(3), 169-191. doi:10.1080/03634523.2014.903333

O'Hara, R. E., Armeli, S., & Tennen, H. (2016). Alcohol and cannabis use among college students: Substitutes or complements? *Addictive Behaviors*, *58*, 1-6. doi:10.1016/j.addbeh.2016.02.004

Orzech, K. M., Salafsky, D. B., & Hamilton, L. A. (2011). The state of sleep among college students at a large public university. *Journal of American College Health: J of ACH*, *59*(7), 612-619. doi:10.1080/07448481.2010.520051

Oswalt, S. B., & Wyatt, T. J. (2013). Sexual health behaviors and sexual orientation in a U.S. national sample of college students. *Archives of Sexual Behavior*, *42*(8), 1561-1572. doi:10.1007/s10508-012-0066-9

Pandya, S. P. (2015). Adolescents, well-being and spirituality: Insights from a spiritual program. *International Journal of Children's Spirituality*, *20*(1), 29-49. doi:10.108 0/1364436X.2014.999230

Paquette, L., Brassard, A., Guérin, A., Fortin-Chevalier, J., & Tanguay-Beaudoin, L. (2014). Effects of a developmental adventure on the self-esteem of college students. *Journal of Experiential Education, 37*(3), 216–231. doi:10.1177/1053825913498372

Park, C., Edmondson, D., & Lee, J. (2012). Development of self-regulation abilities as predictors of psychological adjustment across the first year of college. *Journal of Adult Development, 19*(1), 40–49. doi:10.1007/s10804-011-9133-z

Patrick, M. E., Schulenberg, J. E., & O'Malley, P. M. (2016). High school substance use as a predictor of college attendance, completion, and dropout: A national multi-cohort longitudinal study. *Youth & Society, 48*(3), 425–447.

Sun, P., Jiang, H., Chu, M., & Qian, F. (2014). Gratitude and school well-being among Chinese university students: Interpersonal relationships and social support as mediators. *Social Behavior & Personality: An International Journal, 42*(10), 1689–1698.

Peleg, O., Deutch, C., & Dan, O. (2016). Test anxiety among female college students and its relation to perceived parental academic expectations and differentiation of self. *Learning and Individual Differences, 49*, 428–436. doi:10.1016/j.lindif.2016.06.010

Piazza-Gardner, A., Barry, A. E., & Merianos, A. L. (2016). Assessing drinking and academic performance among a nationally representative sample of college students. *Journal of Drug Issues, 46*(4), 347–353. doi:10.1177/0022042616659757

Ploskonka, R. A., & Servaty-Seib, H. (2015). Belongingness and suicidal ideation in college students. *Journal of American College Health, 63*(2), 81–87.

Plotnikoff, R. C., Costigan, S. A., Williams, R. L., Hutchesson, M. J., Kennedy, S. G., Robards, S. L., . . . Germov, J. (2015). Effectiveness of interventions targeting physical activity, nutrition and healthy weight for university and college students: A systematic review and meta-analysis. *The International Journal of Behavioral Nutrition and Physical Activity, 12*, 45–45. doi:10.1186/s12966-015-0203-7

Polman, R., Borkoles, E., & Nicholls, A. R. (2010). Type D personality, stress, and symptoms of burnout: The influence of avoidance coping and social support. *British Journal of Health Psychology, 15*(3), 681–696.

Posselt, J. R., & Lipson, S. K. (2016). Competition, anxiety, and depression in the college classroom: Variations by student identity and field of study. *Journal of College Student Development, 57*(8), 973–989. doi:10.1353/csd.2016.0094

Rahat, E., & Ilhan, T. (2016). Coping styles, social support, relational self-construal, and resilience in predicting students' adjustment to university life. *Educational Sciences: Theory and Practice, 16*(1), 187–208.

Roa, S. P., Taani, M., Lozano, V., & Kennedy, E. E. (2015). Educating students about suicide: A framework for the use of fotonovelas on college campuses. *College Student Journal, 49*(2), 217–224.

Ray, A. E., Stapleton, J. L., Turrisi, R., & Mun, E. (2014). Drinking game play among first-year college student drinkers: An event-specific analysis of the risk for alcohol use and problems. *American Journal of Drug & Alcohol Abuse, 40*(5), 353–358.

Rayle, A. D., & Myers, J. E. (2004). Counseling adolescents toward wellness: The roles of ethnic identity, acculturation, and mattering. *Professional School Counseling, 8*(1), 81.

Ream, G. L. (2016). The interpersonal-psychological theory of suicide in college student suicide screening. *Suicide & Life-Threatening Behavior, 46*(2), 239–247. doi:10.1111/sltb.12188

Richardson, B., & Shields, J. A. (2015). The real campus sexual assault problem—and how to fix it. *Commentary, 140*(3), 26–31.

Richman, A. R., Webb, M. C., Brinkley, J., & Martin, R. J. (2014). Sexual behaviour and interest in using a sexual health mobile app to help improve and manage college students' sexual health. *Sex Education, 14*(3), 310–322. doi:10.1080/14 681811.2014.889604

Riley, T. J., Kirsch, A. C., Shapiro, J. B., & Conley, C. S. (2016). Examining stress and coping as a mediator for internalizing symptomatology: A comparison between sexual minority and majority first-year college students. *Journal of Adolescence, 49*, 124–133. doi:10.1016/j.adolescence.2016.03.005

Risquez, A., Moore, S., & Morley, M. (2007). Welcome to college? Developing a richer understanding of the transition process for adult first year students using reflective written journals. *Journal of College Student Retention: Research, Theory & Practice, 9*(2), 183–204. doi:10.2190/CS.9.2.d

Romero-Sánchez, M., & Megías, J. L. (2015). How do college students talk about sexual assault? *Journal of Gender Studies, 24*(6), 644–659. doi:10.1080/09589 236.2013.868301

Rosenberger, E. W. (2011). Where I end and you begin: The role of boundaries in college student relationships. *About Campus, 16*(4), 11–19. doi:10.1002/ abc.20069

Ruberman, L. (2014). Challenges in the transition to college: The perspective of the therapist back home. *American Journal of Psychotherapy, 68*(1), 103–115.

Sadigh, M. R., Himmanen, S. A., & Scepansky, J. A. (2014). An investigation of the prevalence of insomnia in college students and its relationship to trait anxiety. *College Student Journal, 48*(3), 397–406.

Sargent, K. S., Krauss, A., Jouriles, E. N., & McDonald, R. (2016). Cyber victimization, psychological intimate partner violence, and problematic mental health outcomes among first-year college students. *Cyberpsychology, Behavior, and Social Networking, 19*(9), 545–550. doi:10.1089/cyber.2016.0115

Scheel, K. R., Prieto, L. R., & Biermann, J. (2011). American Indian college student suicide: Risk, beliefs, and help-seeking preferences. *Counseling Psychology, 24*(4), 277–289.

Sevinç, S., & Gizir, C. A. (2014). Factors negatively affecting university adjustment from the views of first-year university students: The case of Mersin University. *Educational Sciences: Theory & Practice, 14*(4), 1301–1308. doi:10.12738/ estp.2014.4.2081

Shannonhouse, L. R., Myers, J. E., & Sweeney, T. J. (2016). Counseling for wellness. In I. Marini & M. A. Stebnicki (Eds.), *The professional counselor's desk reference* (pp. 617–623). New York, NY: Springer Publishing Co.

Sheppard, M. E., Usdan, S. L., Higginbotham, J. C., & Cremeens-Matthews, J. (2016). Attitudes and descriptive norms of alcohol-related problems as predictors of alcohol use among college students. *Journal of Alcohol & Drug Education, 60*(1), 30–46.

Shurts, W. M., & Myers, J. E. (2008). An examination of liking, love styles, and wellness among emerging adults: Implications for social wellness and development. *ADULTSPAN Journal, 7*(2), 51–68.

Spurgeon, S. L., & Myers, J. E. (2010). African American males: Relationships among racial identity, college type, and wellness. *Journal of Black Studies, 40*(4), 527–543. doi:10.1177/0021934708315153

Spurr, S., Bally, J., Ogenchuk, M., & Walker, K. (2012). A framework for exploring adolescent wellness. *Pediatric Nursing, 38*(6), 320–326.

Spurr, S., Berry, L., & Walker, K. (2013). The meanings older adolescents attach to spirituality. *Journal for Specialists in Pediatric Nursing, 18*(3), 221–232. doi:10.1111/jspn.12028

Standlee, A. (2016). Technology and making-meaning in college relationships: Understanding hyper-connection. *Qualitative Sociology Review, 12*(2), 6–21.

Stanger, S., Abaied, J., & Wagner, C. (2016). Predicting heavy alcohol use in college students: Interactions among socialization of coping, alcohol use onset, and physiological reactivity. *Journal of Studies on Alcohol and Drugs, 77*(3), 483–494.

Sun, P., Jiang, H., Chu, M., & Qian, F. (2014). Gratitude and school well-being among Chinese university students: Interpersonal relationships and social support as mediators. *Social Behavior & Personality: An International Journal, 42*(10), 1689–1698.

Sutfin, E. L., Sparks, A., Pockey, J. R., Suerken, C. K., Reboussin, B. A., Wagoner, K. G., . . . Wolfson, M. (2015). First tobacco product tried: Associations with smoking status and demographics among college students. *Addictive Behaviors, 51*, 152–157. doi:10.1016/j.addbeh.2015.07.022

Sutton, T., & Simons, L. (2015). Sexual assault among college students: Family of origin hostility, attachment, and the hook-up culture as risk factors. *Journal of Child & Family Studies, 24*(10), 2827–2840. doi:10.1007/s10826-014-0087-1

Sylaska, K. M., & Edwards, K. M. (2015). Disclosure experiences of sexual minority college student victims of intimate partner violence. *American Journal of Community Psychology, 55*(3–4), 326–335. doi:10.1007/s10464-015-9717-z

Taylor, D. J., Zimmerman, M. R., Gardner, C. E., Williams, J. M., Grieser, E. A., Tatum, J. I., . . . Ruggero, C. (2014). A pilot randomized controlled trial of the effects of cognitive-behavioral therapy for insomnia on sleep and daytime functioning in college students. *Behavior Therapy, 45*(3), 376–389. doi:10.1016/j.beth.2013.12.010

Tirri, K., & Quinn, B. (2010). Exploring the role of religion and spirituality in the development of purpose: Case studies of purposeful youth. *British Journal of Religious Education, 32*(3), 201–214. doi:10.1080/01416200.2010.498607

Trautwein, C., & Bosse, E. (2017). The first year in higher education—critical requirements from the student perspective. *Higher Education, 73*(3), 371–387. doi:10.1007/s10734-016-0098-5

Tresno, F., Ito, Y., & Mearns, J. (2012). Self-injurious behavior and suicide attempts among Indonesian college students. *Death Studies, 36*(7), 627–639. doi:10.1080/07481187.2011.604464

Uz, C., & Cagiltay, K. (2015). Social interactions and games. *Digital Education Review, (27)*, 1–12.

Van Dyke, C. J., Glenwick, D. S., Cecero, J. J., & Se-Kang Kim. (2009). The relationship of religious coping and spirituality to adjustment and psychological distress in urban early adolescents. *Mental Health, Religion & Culture, 12*(4), 369–383. doi:10.1080/13674670902737723

Vargas, P. A., Flores, M., & Robles, E. (2014). Sleep quality and body mass index in college students: The role of sleep disturbances. *Journal of American College Health, 62*(8), 534–541. doi:10.1080/07448481.2014.933344

Wang, M., Lightsey, O. R., Tran, K. K., & Bonaparte, T. S. (2013). Examining suicide protective factors among black college students. *Death Studies, 37*(3), 228–247. doi:10.1080/07481187.2011.623215

Wasylkiw, L. (2016). Students' perspectives on pathways to university readiness and adjustment. *Journal of Education and Training Studies, 4*(3), 28–39.

Weybright, E. H., Cooper, B. R., Beckmeyer, J., Bumpus, M. F., Hill, L. G., & Agley, J. (2016). Moving beyond drinking to have a good time: A person-centered approach to identifying reason typologies in legal-aged college student drinkers. *Prevention Science: The Official Journal of the Society for Prevention Research, 17*(6), 679–688. doi:10.1007/s11121-016-0658-z

Womble, M. N., Labbé, E. E., Shelley-Tremblay, J., & Norrell, P. (2014). Regular exercise adoption: Psychosocial factors influencing college students. *Journal of Sport Behavior, 37*(2), 203–219.

Xie, X. (2016). Research on influence of physical exercise and nutrition intervention on physical quality of college students. *Carpathian Journal of Food Science & Technology, 8*(3), 111–119.

Yahia, N., Brown, C. A., Rapley, M., & Chung, M. (2016). Level of nutrition knowledge and its association with fat consumption among college students. *BMC Public Health, 16*(1), 1047–1047.

Yan, Z., Berger, B. G., Tobar, D. A., & Cardina, B. J. (2015). Comparison of American and Chinese college students' reasons for exercise, exercise enjoyment and self-efficacy. *International Journal of Applied Sports Sciences, 27*(1), 43–50.

Ye, L., Hutton Johnson, S., Keane, K., Manasia, M., & Gregas, M. (2015). Napping in college students and its relationship with nighttime sleep. *Journal of American College Health: J of ACH, 63*(2), 88–97. doi:10.1080/07448481.2014.983926

Young, C. M., Neighbors, C., DiBello, A. M., Sharp, C., Zvolensky, M. J., & Lewis, M. A. (2016). Coping motives moderate efficacy of personalized normative feedback among heavy drinking U.S. college students. *Journal of Studies on Alcohol and Drugs, 77*(3), 495–499.

Zhou, X., Zhu, H, Zhang, B., & Cai, T. (2013). Perceived social support as moderator of perfectionism, depression, and anxiety in college students. *Social Behavior & Personality: An International Journal, 41*(7), 1141–1152. doi:10.2224/sbp.2013.41.7.1141

Zou, Z., Liu, Y., Xie, J., & Huang, X. (2016). Aerobic exercise as a potential way to improve self-control after ego-depletion in healthy female college students. *Frontiers in Psychology, 7*, 501–501. doi:10.3389/fpsyg.2016.00501

www.ingramcontent.com/pod-product-compliance
Lightning Source LLC
Chambersburg PA
CBHW061745270326
41928CB00011B/2376